Paddle Your Own Boat:

10 Rules that Guarantee Career Success

Paddle Your Own Boat:

10 Rules that Guarantee Career Success

Vernon L. Williams

Empowerment Publishers
Columbia, Maryland

Library of Congress Cataloging-in-publication Data

Williams, Vernon L.

Paddle Your Own Boat: 10 Rules that Guarantee Career Success

ISBN 0-9777338-3-1

Published By Empowerment Publishers

This book is available at special quantity discounts to use as premiums and sales promotions, or for use in corporate and government training programs. For more information please go to www.vernonwilliams.net.

Other Books by Vernon L. Williams

o Why Employees Fail to Meet Performance
   Expectations & How to Fix the Problem

o 425 Ways to Stretch Your $$$$

Available at **www.vernonwilliams.net**

Dedication

This book is dedicated to my wife, Gayle, who has always been my biggest fan.

Acknowledgments

I want to express my thanks to wife, Gayle, for proofreading the manuscript and offering ideas for improvement. I also want to thank Cindy Durham for her help in proofreading the manuscript.

Contents

Preface

As I interact with employees, I find they are quite candid in expressing their concerns, which generally fall into one of three areas:

1. They feel "trapped" in a job they do not like.

A recent survey of 180,000 white-collar and blue-collar workers revealed that 80% of them do not like their jobs.

2. They would like to advance in their career but have fallen short in their efforts to make it happen.

3. They are worried about being laid off.

This, of course, is a real possibility. As organizations scramble to get leaner and more efficient, they are making greater use of part-time, freelance and contract workers - all at the expense of full-time employees. Even the federal government, which used to be the model for job security, has created the Workforce Restructuring Office to assist federal employees who are victims of a Reduction in Force (RIF) initiative.

The strategies I have outlined in this book will help you survive and thrive in the workforce, whether you are seeking a new position, attempting to advance in your career or fretting over the possibility of being RIF'D.

Having done more than ten years of research, I have concluded that successful people adhere to ten rules. By sharing these rules, I hope that you will, as one recent seminar attendee put it, change your life forever.

Good luck to you as you pursue your career goals.

1

Take 100% Responsibility

If you want to be successful, there is only one person you can look at as being responsible. That's you!

—Alan Page, NFL Hall of Famer and current Associate Justice of the Minnesota Supreme Court

When it comes to pursuing career goals, some people "get it" and others do not. Those who "get it" operate with the idea, "If it's to be, it's up to me." They refuse to delegate responsibility for their career to Human Resources (HR), their boss, their boss' boss or to anyone else. They are "victors," which the dictionary defines as "winners in a contest or battle."

On the other hand, those who do not "get it" are "victims," which the dictionary defines as "someone who experiences misfortune and feels helpless to do anything about it." They allow others to control their career. Then, when they don't achieve their goals, they blame others and they feel helpless to do anything about the situation. During my 10 years of conducting seminars, I have kept a list of some of the blaming statements victims use most often:

"I could be further along in my career if I had a better boss."

"They didn't give me the position because I don't have a degree."

"My boss won't recommend/release me."

"It's not what you know, but who you know that enables you to get ahead around here."

"I guess I will wait and hope that something positive happens."

"I have tried several times. They just won't promote me. I am giving up."

The act of blaming others is not new. The first recorded example of this was in the Bible when God told Adam he could eat from every tree except the Tree of Knowledge. Of course, Adam ate from the forbidden tree. When God asked if he had done so, did Adam step up and take responsibility? No. Instead he said, "The woman you gave to be with me, she (Eve) gave me of the tree, and I ate." Thus the pattern of blaming others had begun. We first see evidence of this early in life. If a child breaks something he or she is likely to blame a brother or sister. Later, if the child receives a poor grade in a particular class, he or she blames the teacher for not liking him or her. At work, employees blame their bosses if they don't receive good performance evaluations. People sue tobacco companies after contracting lung cancer from smoking. Others sue bartenders after receiving a Driving While Intoxicated (DWI) citation. There is a song called "Blame it on the Bossa Nova". There is even a website called www.ShiftTheBlame.com.

A Chinese proverb says "A journey of 1,000 miles begins

with a single step." If you are to achieve your career goals the first step is to choose to be a "victor" and not a "victim". There are huge differences:

A "victim" says:	A "victor" says:
"I could be further along in my career if I had a better boss."	"If I am to succeed in my career, it is up to me to make it happen."
"I am trapped in this job that I do not like because I do not have a degree."	"If a college degree is necessary in order to achieve my goals, I will get a college degree."
"My boss won't recommend/release me."	"I own my career. It is up to me to find a way to achieve my goal."
"It's not **what** you know, but **who** you know that enables you to get ahead."	"Even if it means going outside my comfort zone, I will build relationships with people who can help me achieve my career goals."
"I guess I will just wait and hope that something positive happens."	"I will get over the notion that good things come to those who wait. I will act now to accomplish my goals."
"I have tried several times. They just won't promote me. I am giving up."	"Obviously, I have not used the appropriate strategy. I will analyze the situation and use a different approach."

You can choose to be a victim or victor. As Zig Ziglar said, "You are free to choose, but the choices you make today will determine what you will have, be and do in the tomorrow of your life."

How to move from victim to victor:

In my seminars I ask participants three questions:

1. What can you gain by taking responsibility for your career?

They list things like feeling more in control, having a better chance of achieving their goals, greater job satisfaction and improved self-esteem.

(Write **your** answers in the space provided below.)

_____

_____

_____

_____

_____

_____

2. What can you gain by giving someone else responsibility for your career?

Invariably, they come up with things like frustration, anger, disappointment and depression.

(Write **your** answer in the space provided below.)

_____

_____

_____

_____

_____

_____

3. In light of the positive results you can gain by taking responsibility for your career, why do you give that responsibility to someone else?

It suddenly gets very quiet in the room. Then somebody finally says it – the reason they don't take responsibility is because of **FEAR.** They go on to say if they take responsibility and things don't turn out as they would like, they would have to admit they are lacking in some area. So rather than risk facing their own shortcomings, they do not make the effort and simply blame their boss, the organization or even their co-workers for their lack of achievement.

Since fear has been called the "dark room where negatives are developed," you must overcome it in order to achieve your career goals.

How to overcome fear:

1. Acknowledge it.

As Dr. Phil says, "You cannot change what you don't acknowledge." Failure to acknowledge fear means you will be stuck with your rationalizations (i.e. "My boss did not tell me about the position." "They don't tell you anything around here." "You have to be part of the "In Crowd" to get anywhere around here." "My supervisor will not release me", etc.) However, once you acknowledge fear you are on your way to managing it, rather than the other way around.

2. Recognize fear as a normal emotion.

All of us have fear to some extent. It is only when it prevents you from taking action that is in your best interest that it becomes a huge negative. As Dale Galloway said, "People who refuse to move ahead because they are afraid of failure do not protect their self-respect; they lose it."

3. Ask yourself: What is the worst thing that can happen if I take responsibility for my career? Accept that.

Fear invariably causes you to project a negative outcome. However, once you are prepared to accept the potential negative outcome, fear no longer has power over you. So, if you are willing to accept the possibility that you might not achieve your goal, (in which case you would be no worse off than you are right now) that frees you from fear and enables you to build towards achieving your goals. At that point confidence has triumphed over fear.

4. Review the list of positive things you can gain by taking responsibility for your career.

Fear causes you to believe only negative things can happen. However, a number of positive things can happen. Review your answers to Question Number 1 under How to move from victim to victor on page 18.

5. Draw confidence your accomplishments.

Look back over your life and relive your successes. I can remember winning a school-wide spelling bee in the 8th grade, being promoted to sergeant in the U.S. Army at age 19, achieving the highest Grade Point Average (GPA) in English my freshman year in college, getting a Master's Degree and starting my own business. When I think of those accomplishments, it gives me confidence that I can achieve anything that I set out to do. The same holds true for you.

List your accomplishments:

_____

_____

_____

_____

6. Visualize achieving your career goal.

A very common technique among professional golfers is to pause for a few seconds before they swing their club. During this time they visualize the ball going into the cup. Once they have this positive outcome programmed into their mind, it becomes much easier to achieve the desired result.

So once you have identified your goal, visualize yourself in the new role. Imagine how you are dressed and how people are responding to you. Have a friend take a picture of you in your new surroundings. (You may have to come in on Saturday or stay late one day in order to do this.) Post copies of the picture in conspicuous places where you can see it regularly, i.e. on the refrigerator, on the bathroom mirror and on the dashboard of your car.

7. Act "as if" you are not afraid.

William Glasser said: "If you want to change what you think, change the way you act." So ask yourself: How would I act if I were not afraid? Then start acting that way. As the old saying goes, "Fake it till you make it".

8. Recognize that achieving any degree of success involves taking risks.

As James Conant said, "Behold the turtle. He only gets ahead when he sticks his neck out.

9. Tune out others' negative remarks.

Keep away from people who belittle your ambitions.

—Mark Twain

Sadly, there are always those who will try to deter you from achieving your goals. They might say things like, "You know they are not going to promote you." Tuning out those remarks prevents other people from robbing you of your dreams.

10. Avoid negative self-talk.

While negative talk by others can sabotage your efforts, negative self-talk poses an even bigger threat. All of us talk to ourselves. The problem is that much of what we tell ourselves is negative. Let me give you an example. Some time ago, a friend of mine set a goal of paying off her credit card debt within 24 months. After setting the goal, she started saying things to herself like, "I've always been in debt – I will never get out." It didn't take long for her negative self-talk to overwhelm her. Eventually she gave up on her longtime dream of being debt-free. It took many counseling sessions before she learned to stop engaging in negative self-talk and move on with paying off her debt. Today, she is not only debt-free, but she conducts workshops to help other women develop and implement a plan for paying off their debts. So make sure your self-talk is positive.

11. Associate with people who have the same goal as you.

For example, if your goal is to earn your college degree, but due to family and work obligations the only way you can do it is through an online university, connect with others who are doing the same thing. They will help you maintain the necessary momentum to reach your goal.

12. Draw encouragement from others who overcame fear.

When her husband committed suicide in 1963, Katherine Graham suddenly found herself thrust into the role of chief executive officer (CEO) of the Washington Post. By her own admission, she had very little idea of what she was supposed to do and she was scared. However, she attacked the job with enthusiasm and sought to learn and apply appropriate management techniques. On June 15, 1971, when she began selling shares of the company, the price per share was $6.50. When she stepped down as CEO on May 9, 1991, the price per share had risen to $222, a gain of 3,315 percent.

When asked how she had overcome her fear and achieved such phenomenal success, Mrs. Graham said, "What I essentially did was put one foot in front of the other, shut my eyes and step off the ledge. The surprise was that I landed on my feet." I would say Katherine Graham operated on Nancy Anderson's theory that "courage is not the absence of fear, but the ability to act in spite of fear."

13. Avoid thinking about how long it will take to achieve your goal.

For example, if you need to go back to school, don't think in terms of the number of years it will take to complete your degree. Just focus of the first class you will take. Once you have completed that, focus on the next class, and so on.

14. Get over the Holier-than-Thou Syndrome.

I recommend to my workshop attendees that they target a specific department within their organization and approach the head of that department, introduce themselves and explain how they can help them achieve their goals. Most attendees are intimidated about doing this. I tell them to remember that the department head is human just like they are. Both of you get up and get dressed and go to work each day. Both of you have skills. Finally, I tell them to disregard the fact that the department head is at a higher organizational level than they are.

15. Get started now.

As Dale Carnegie said, "Not taking action breads fear and doubt. Taking actions breeds confidence and courage. So, if you want to conquer fear, do not sit home and think about it. Go out and get busy."

Theresa's story is an example of what can happen when you take this approach. She had worked for her government agency for more than 20 years. Despite all of her complaints about never having gotten promoted, she had not taken any action to make it happen. Instead she, like many of her co-workers, had fallen into the trap of blaming others and making excuses.

When Theresa attended my two-day workshop, initially she held fast to her belief that others were responsible for her career. I pointed out that by allowing someone else to control her career, she was giving away all her power.

By the end of the first day Theresa had begun to buy into the notion that her career was her responsibility. When she came back for the second day, she became totally sold on the fact that she was responsible and had the power to make changes, and she was eager to learn specific strategies she could employ to advance her career.

When she left the workshop she was very excited about applying the strategies she had learned. I found out later that she had been promoted two salary grades before the year was out.

ACTION PLAN

I will implement the following ideas:

1. _____.

2. _____.

3. _____.

4. _____.

5. _____.

2

Develop and Maintain A Positive Attitude

There is very little difference in people. But that little difference makes a big difference. The little difference is ATTITUDE. The big difference is whether it is positive or negative.

—W. Clement Stone

The dictionary defines "attitude" as "the way we see the events, people and circumstances in our life."

Your attitude determines how you feel, what you think, what you say and what you do. Therefore, it has a powerful impact on whether or not you achieve your career goals. This impact was demonstrated in a Harvard University study which concluded that **85%** of the reason that people get a job and get ahead can be attributed to attitude and **15%** of the reason can be attributed to technical skill.

As Zig Ziglar says, "It's your attitude, not your aptitude that determines your altitude."

The bad news is that, despite its importance, studies show that many people have a negative attitude.

The good news is that you can change your attitude from negative to positive. In so doing, you can change your life.

As psychologist William James said: "The most important discovery of my lifetime is that people can change their lives by changing their attitude."

How to change your attitude from negative to positive:

1. Take 100 % responsibility for your attitude.

"Responsibility" is made up of two words: "Response" and "Ability." That means that, in any situation, you have the ability to choose your response.

Let's look at some examples:

Mary's boss gives her some corrective feedback. Mary gets mad. She tells her coworkers that the boss made her mad. Mary's performance deteriorates even further.

Now let's look at two other examples:

When Ben Carson was in grade school the other kids laughed it him. In fact, they labeled him the dumbest kid in the 5th grade. With urging from his mother, Ben set out to improve his performance. Today, he is one of the most renowned neurosurgeons in the world.

As a youngster, Les Brown was labeled "educable mentally retarded".

Les took the attitude that "someone else's opinion of me does not have to become my reality." He worked extremely hard to develop his skills as a speaker and today he earns $20,000 per hour as one of America's top motivational speakers.

In every case, there was a stimulus over which the person had no control. However, while the person could not control the stimulus, he or she had complete control over their response. While Mary chose to get mad and allow her performance to slip even more, Ben and Les chose to use the negative comments as a springboard to success.

So, if you are to change your attitude from negative to positive, you must begin by taking 100% responsibility.

2. Change your thinking.

"Every thought we think is creating our future."

—Louise L Hay

Here is how your thinking creates your future:

You have a thought, the thought leads to an image, the image leads to an emotion, the emotion leads to a choice, the choice leads to a habit, and habits determine your destiny.

Let's look at an example:

A job opening is announced and it means a promotion.

Bill thinks: There is really no use applying for the position. They have already decided whom they are going to promote.

The image Bill sees: Another person being selected for the position.

The emotion Bill feels: Hopeless.

Bill's choice: He applies for the position but, since he has decided he has no chance of getting it, he follows his usual pattern of doing a poor job of completing the application. As a result, Bill does not get selected for the position. He says, "I knew it."

Let's look at another example:

A job opening is announced and it means a promotion.

Jill thinks: This position is open to the best-qualified candidate. I am the best qualified candidate.

The image Jill sees: She is in the position, carrying out all of the duties and collecting a bigger paycheck.

The emotion Jill feels: Encouraged.

Jill's choice: As is her custom, she reads the vacancy announcement carefully and completes the application, making sure she matches her qualifications to what the hiring manager is looking for. She makes the Best Qualified list, gets invited for an interview, prepares for the interview, and does a terrific job of "selling herself" to the interview panel. Jill gets the promotion.

The difference in Bill and Jill is their thoughts.

Like Bill, Jill had formed a habit. But unlike Bill, Jill makes it a habit of thinking positively, preparing for opportunities and then going after those opportunities.

According to studies by the National Science Foundation the average person has at least 12,000 thoughts per day. Since we are such creatures of habit, 95% of the thoughts we have today are the same ones we had yesterday, the day before and the day before that.

Those same studies show that at least 50% of those thoughts are negative. So you can see that most people repeat the same 6,000 negative thoughts day after day.

How to change your thoughts from negative to positive:

All of us have the ability to have a thought and be aware of it at the time we are having it. Because of this awareness, you can change what you think about. Let me illustrate how this is possible. When I say "Go," start counting backward from 10. When you reach 5, stop counting and start thinking about where you would like to go on vacation. Okay, "Go." Were you able to stop counting at 5? I am sure you were. What you did was change your thinking. Let us look at three ways you can change your thinking and how you can apply each:

Method	How to apply the method
The straightforward approach	Immediately recognize the thought and replace it with a different one. You just used this approach when you were counting backward from 10.
The cost-benefit analysis	List the advantages and the disadvantages of the thought. If the disadvantages outweigh the advantages, replace the thought with a positive one. For an example of how this works, review Rule 1 – Take 100% responsibility. Pay special attention to questions 1 and 2 under How to move from victim to victor.
Examine the evidence	Instead of assuming that your thought is true, examine the evidence for it. If the evidence does not support the thought, replace it with a positive one. See the example of Carla below

I had an experience recently that involved the examine the evidence method. I was leading a workshop on Taking Charge of Your Career. One of the participants, Carla, said, "It's impossible to get promoted around here unless you are related to one of the executives." I asked her if she was saying that no one had ever gotten promoted unless they were related to an executive. After thinking about it, she said that was not true. She acknowledged that the evidence did not support her contention.

In order for the positive thought to be effective, however, you must believe it.

I read an Archie comic strip in which Jughead sought Archie's advice because he was lacking confidence. The following exchange took place between the two of them:

Jughead: Archie, I believe I will fail at what I want to do.

Archie: Just tell yourself that you can do it.

Jughead: That's not going to work.

Archie: Why won't it work?

Jughead: Because I know what a liar I am.

I don't think Jughead benefited from Archie's advice.

The poem "Changing Your Thinking" puts all of this into perspective.

Changing Your Thinking
—Author Unknown

When you change your thinking,
you change your beliefs;
When you change your beliefs,
you change your expectations;
When you change your expectations,
you change your attitude;
When you change your attitude,
you change your behavior;
When you change your behavior,
you change your performance;
When you change your performance;
you change your life.

3. Speak positive words.

The words you use can elevate you or deflate you.
Choose words that do the former. Let me give you some
examples:

Instead of saying: I am overwhelmed.

Say: I am challenged.

Instead of saying: I failed.

Say: I had a temporary setback.

Instead of saying: I am confused.

Say: I am curious.

Instead of saying: I was laid off/downsized/fired.

Say: I am currently in career transition.

Instead of saying: I feel stupid.

Say: I feel temporarily unresourceful.

4. Change what you feed your mind.

Your mind grows based on what you feed it. If you listen to television news or read a newspaper many of the stories are about murder, unemployment, war, robbery and rape. In order to balance that negativity:

o   Listen to inspirational tapes.

o   Read inspirational books such as The Bible.

o   Listen to inspirational music.

o   Read inspiring stories in magazines.

o   Read biographies of people who have overcome obstacles in order to achieve success. Examples are:

> o   Fanny Crosby - Despite becoming blind at 6 weeks old, she went on to write more than 8,000 songs.

> o   Henry Ford – He went bankrupt twice but overcame it and went on to found the Ford Motor Company.

- Ray Kroc suffered from diabetes, was heavily into debt and worked several jobs before founding McDonald's.

- Use the Internet – Type "Inspiration" and you will see many Web sites that have inspiring stories and quotes. Several of them will send you a free newsletter or daily positive quotes.

5. Act the way you want to be until you become the way you are acting.

William Glasser said, "If you want to change your attitude, start with a change in behavior."

You can prove this to yourself. If you are feeling discouraged, stand up, pull your shoulders back, hold your head up, smile and start singing your favorite song. Within a few minutes your body will trick your mind and you will begin to feel encouraged.

Og Mandino talked about how he used his actions to control his emotions this way:

If I feel depressed I will sing.
If I feel sad I will laugh.
If I feel ill I will double my labor.
If I feel fear I will plunge ahead.
If I feel inferior I will wear new garments.
If I feel uncertain I will raise my voice.
If I feel poverty I will think of wealth to come.
If I feel incompetent I will think of past success.
If I feel insignificant I will remember my goals.
Today I will be the master of my emotions.

6. Smile or laugh.

Studies show that Preschool children smile or laugh 300 times per day. By age 35, that number drops to 15 times per day. Smiling or laughing offers many benefits. For example it helps you:

    a. Build confidence.

    b. Build relationships.

Feeling abused by patients and disrespected by doctors, two nurses decided to quit their job. So they gave their two-week notices. Since they were only going to be there two more weeks, they decided to smile and be pleasant no matter how others treated them. After a few days they started to notice that the more they smiled and were pleasant, the more people were pleasant to them. The patients began saying please and thank you. The doctors started telling them what a terrific job they were doing and how much they appreciated them.

The nurses had learned a valuable lesson - the world reflects what you give out.

    c. Lose weight.

A hearty laugh burns up 3 ½ calories.

    d. Boost your immune system.

There is a proverb that says: A merry heart does good like medicine but a broken spirit dries the bones.

Scientific evidence shows that good spirits lead to more harmones, hormones produce white blood cells, white blood cells fight infection.

e. Lower your blood pressure.

f. Relieve stress.

7. Help someone who cannot return the favor.

When things are not going well, it is easy to have a "Pity Party" and feel sorry for yourself. Since all of the focus is on you, this can cause your attitude to sink like a rock. To avoid this, do something for someone where there is no chance they can pay you back.

In 1991 my wife and I began visiting terminally ill people in their homes, in hospitals and in nursing homes. It started with AIDS patients and quickly moved to people who were suffering from any type of terminal illness. All of them expressed a tremendous appreciation for our willingness to spend time with them, particularly since there was neither a monetary gain nor any chance of them returning the favor. While I am sure they genuinely appreciated the time we spent with them, it is impossible for me to describe the satisfaction and joy we have received from knowing we were helping without expecting anything in return.

8. Make a "Quit" list.

We are told, "Winners never quit". Actually winners do quit. They quit things that are preventing them from accomplishing their goals.

Some things you might consider quitting:

o   Viewing yourself as a victim.

o   Dwelling on past disappointments.

o   Worrying about what others are doing.

o   Making alibis.

As Eric Hoffer said, "There are many who find a good alibi far more attractive than an achievement." Some typical alibis are: I was going to go back to school but.., I was going to do some networking but.., I was going to update my resume but..

o   Worrying about something that may not even happen.

It has been said worrying is like being in a rocking chair. It gives you something to do, but it does not get you anywhere. Besides, studies show that 90% of what people worry about never happens. As Montaigne said: "My life has been full of misfortune, most of which never happened."

How to control worry:

o   In any situation ask yourself – What is the worst thing that can happen? Accept that. Move on.

o   Adopt the attitude that yesterday is a cancelled check, tomorrow is a promissory note, but today is ready cash. Spend it wisely.

o   Remember Les Brown's two rules to life:

1. Don't sweat the small stuff.

2. It's all small stuff.

9. Count your blessings.

In her best-selling book, Simple *Abundance*: *A Daybook of Comfort and Joy,* Sarah Ban Breathnach wrote:

"Real life is not always going to be perfect or go our way, but the recurring acknowledgement of **what is working** in our lives can help us not only to survive but surmount our difficulties."

List the things in your life for which you are thankful.

_____

_____

_____

_____

_____

_____

_____

_____

_____

_____

_____

_____

Review the list every day.

Add new things to the list.

10. Associate with positive people.

All of us have seen the sign that says: "It's hard to soar like an eagle when you are surrounded by turkeys." That is more than a clever saying. Studies show that the biggest single influence on whether or not you are successful is the people with whom you associate. While negative people are toxic and can suck the life out of you, positive people can spur you to new heights. So, which kind of people do you spend your time with?

Take a sheet of paper and make two columns. On one side write "Yes" people. These are the people who lift your spirits and offer encouragement. On the other side of the paper write "No" people. These are the people who are negative about everything, never try to achieve anything and belittle you if you talk about going back to school, getting a promotion, buying a new house, etc.

For me some of the "Yes" people are:

o My wife Gayle who, despite many illnesses, manages to smile, keep a great attitude and support me unconditionally.

o My two mothers-in-law (Elizabeth Budd and Martina Beckett), who always encourage me and believe that I can do anything that I decide I want to do.

o Steve Gallison, who is always willing to serve as a "sounding board" and to give wise counsel.

o Kathryn Troutman, the owner of The Resume Place, who has shared many ideas on publishing and marketing my books.

If you have people like this in your life, spend time with them and pick their brain. Ask for their methods and follow their example.

If you don't have people like this in your life, find them.

11. Look for the opportunities in adversity.

"Every opportunity has a difficulty and every difficulty has an opportunity."

—Sidlow Baxter

When something happens that we consider negative, it "can" rob us of energy, enthusiasm and drive. I say, "can" because, remember, we choose our response. We can choose to wallow in self-pity or we can look for the opportunities.

A parable is told of a farmer who owned an old mule. One day, the mule fell into the farmer's dry well. The farmer heard the mule braying from the bottom of the dry well. After carefully assessing the situation, although he sympathized with the mule, the farmer decided that neither the mule nor the well was worth saving. Instead, he called his neighbors together and told them what had happened and enlisted them to help haul dirt to bury the old mule in the well and put him out of his misery.

Initially, as the dirt landed on him, the old mule was in a panic. But as the farmer and his neighbors continued shoveling more and more dirt and the dirt hit his back the mule had a thought.

It dawned on him that every time a shovel load of dirt landed on his back, he could SHAKE IT OFF AND STEP UP! This he did, shovel full after shovel full. "SHAKE IT OFF AND STEP UP! SHAKE IT OFF AND STEP UP! No matter how painful the dirt was when it hit his back, or how distressing the situation seemed, the old mule refused to panic and just kept SHAKING IT OFF AND STEPPING UP.

You are right. It was not long before the old mule, though battered and exhausted, stepped triumphantly over the wall of the well. The situation that seemed at first like it would bury him, actually blessed him, all because of the manner in which he handled this adversity.

I used that approach when I got the word that, after 23 years with a company, I (and 5,000 others) was being downsized. While in career transition, I looked for the opportunity in the situation.

I decided to SHAKE IT OFF AND STEP UP by becoming an author and motivational speaker.

ACTION PLAN

I will implement the following ideas:

1. _____.

2. _____.

3. _____.

4. _____.

5._____.

3

Excel In Your Current Position

Nobody gets to run the mill by doing run-of-the-mill work.

—Thomas J. Frye

Since people who mishandle their current position do not get promoted to a higher position, your goal must be to excel where you are.

How to excel:

1. Understand your employer's mission.

Every organization has a mission – the reason it exists.

Quality Inns' mission is "To pursue excellence and become the most recognized, respected, and admired lodging chain in the world."

Ryder System's mission is "To be the growing leader in providing high quality transportation support services to business customers."

The Social Security Administration's mission is "To advance the economic security of the nation's people through compassionate and vigilant leadership in shaping and managing America's Social Security programs."

Write your employer's mission.

_____

_____

_____

_____

_____

_____

2. Understand how your job helps your employer accomplish the mission.

If you understand the "big picture" you are more likely to be motivated to do a better job. However, 74% of employees surveyed said they did not understand their organization's mission or how their activities impacted it.

Write how your job helps your organization accomplish its mission.

_____

_____

_____

_____

_____

There is a story about a man who saw two workers breaking granite, and he stopped to talk. When he asked one worker, "What are you doing?" The man replied, "I'm trying to break this granite."

He said to the other one, "What are you doing?"

The second worker paused to consider the question, stuck out his chest and said proudly, "I am part of a team that is building a cathedral."

Which man do you think did the better job?

3. Understand your supervisor's expectations.

In order to succeed in helping your employer accomplish the mission, you and your supervisor must be in lock-step agreement on your duties (**what** you are expected to do) and the performance objectives (**how well** are you expected to perform the duties)

Example:

Job Duty   Performance Objective

Prepare service orders   Achieve 98 % accuracy

As a first step in this process of reaching agreement on duties and objectives, use Figure 3.1 – Job Duty Worksheet on page 48 to record what you perceive to be your duties and the performance objectives for each duty.

Figure 3.1

Job Duty Worksheet

Job Duty #1 (What)   Performance Objective (How Well)

Job Duty #2 (What)   Performance Objective (How Well)

Job Duty #3 (What)   Performance Objective (How Well)

Job Duty #4 (What)   Performance Objective (How Well)

Having developed what you think are your duties and the associated performance objectives, the next step is to meet with your supervisor to reach agreement. It does not matter that some of what you have written will get changed, new things will get added or some things will get deleted. The important thing is that you and your supervisor leave the meeting with a written agreement on what you are expected to do and how well you are expected to do it.

4. Go beyond your basic duties.

This is sometimes called providing "value-added" services. Let me give you an example of an employee who did that.

Massachusetts was facing a 460 million dollar budget deficit. The governor was talking about laying off employees and raising taxes to eliminate the deficit.

Kathleen Betts, a single mom who worked in the Medicaid Department, decided to see how she could help alleviate the situation. On her own initiative she began taking regulations home at night to study them. After months of study she found that the federal government was under-reimbursing the state. When the auditors examined the records they found that the total amount of the under-reimbursement came to 489 million dollars.

The budget crisis was resolved. Kathleen was named ABC TV News Person of the Week and her picture appeared on the front cover of the New York Times.

What added value can you bring to your employer?

Think of how you can cut costs, improve efficiency, increase sales, improve customer satisfaction, etc.

_____

_____

_____

_____

_____

_____

_____

_____

5. Become an expert in your field.

Al had just begun his career as corporate supervisor. One day, his boss pulled him aside and gave me some of the best advice he would ever receive. He said, "If you want to really excel around here, or in any other job, become an expert." He went on to tell Al there are two advantages to being an expert:

> a. It increases his value to his current and future employers. He quoted Ralph Waldo Emerson, who said, "If a man can write a better book, preach a better sermon, or make a better mousetrap than his neighbor, though he builds his house in the woods, the world will beat a path to his door."

> b. With his increased value he would be indispensable and thus able to command more in compensation.

By this time, Al's boss definitely had his attention. However, Al had just graduated from college and newly hired into management. He didn't know much about the company, so he asked his boss to suggest an area in which he could become an expert. The boss' answer startled Al. He said, "That is entirely up to you. Just pick an area and become an expert in it."

Recognizing that I was an expert in training managers, Al sought my advice. So let me share the steps I recommended that Al follow in order to become recognized as an expert:

a. Choose the area in which you want to become an expert.

It is best to pick a field that you are interested in. Beyond that, it could be a field in which no one has yet recognized the need for an expert, or it could be a field that everyone knows they need, but no one has been willing to invest the time and effort into becoming an expert.

b. Develop knowledge that is superior to 99% of the people.

This, of course, requires a great deal of study. Read everything you can get your hands on related to the subject. Interview others who have some knowledge about certain aspects of the field.

c. Start thinking of yourself as an expert.

The first person you have to convince that you are an expert is you. If you don't believe it, no one else will.

d. Tell others that you are an expert.

This is why every waiter in Los Angeles will tell you he or she is an actor, even though they have not landed a part.

e. Take on additional work assignments in your area of expertise.

This allows you to both continue to build and showcase your expertise.

f. Write an article for your organization's newsletter.

You get to show your expertise and your writing skills to a wide audience. Someone in that audience may be looking for someone with your skills. Include a picture of yourself along with the article, if possible.

g. Conduct a workshop for fellow employees.

h. Speak up in meetings.

Offer well-thought out solutions at the appropriate time.

i. Teach a class at a community college.

You won't make a lot of money, but you will gain valuable experience in talking about your subject. You'll also make valuable contacts, and you can add the experience to your resume.

j. Write an article for your local newspaper.

k. Write an article for your industry trade journal.

l. Write articles for Web sites.

Editors are always looking for quality content. Go to http://www.ideamarketers.com   for a listing of online publications to which you can submit your work.

m. Establish a blog.

Blog, which is short for Weblog, is a Web site that takes on the form of an on-line journal. You can write articles on your area of expertise. The articles, known as "posts", form a separate page on the Internet.   Since many people read the articles, they could lead to some great opportunities.

It is easy to establish a blog. You can literally set one up in five minutes. It is also extremely easy to add information to it. You just log in, type what you want to say, post it, and you're done.

There is little of no cost involved. Go to services like www.blogger or www.typepad.com to get details on costs and how to establish your blog.

n. Ask for testimonial letters.

Since testimonials carry a lot weight in influencing opinions, ask people who can attest to your expertise to put it in writing.

o. Give free speeches and seminars.

The chamber of commerce and other professional groups are always looking for speakers. Give free seminars and speeches.

p. Contact radio and TV stations to arrange to be interviewed.

Local media are always looking for experts to interview on a variety of topics. Send them your bio and credentials and follow up with a call to arrange a time for them to interview you.

q. Establish your own Web site.

This will give you wide exposure. Include lots of free information on your area of expertise. Include a picture of yourself.

r. Write a book.

This will go a long way in establishing you as an expert. Include quotes on the back cover from knowledgeable individuals who can attest to your expertise.

After some thought, Al decided to become expert in labor relations, and he followed many of the steps I have outlined. It took a lot of hard work, but it paid off. Today, as a recognized expert, he charges outrageous consultant fees.

6. Develop your organizational savvy.

Forget the organization chart and the operating manual. Get to know how things "really" work in the organization. What are the priorities? How do decisions get made? What kinds of people get promoted?

7. Develop a resource network.

In today's fast-changing workplace it is almost impossible for you to have all of the knowledge you need in order to perform your duties. This means you must constantly seek to develop relationships with people who can fill in the gaps between what you know and what you need to know. The first step is to make a list of the things you need to know but do not know. The second step is to identify people who can provide the information. Use Figure 3.2 - Resource Network on page 56 to complete this activity.

Figure 3.2

RESOURCE NETWORK

Things you need to know but do not know:	People who can provide the knowledge:

The third step is to begin building relationships. For maximum effectiveness, you should also look for ways to be a resource to others. In fact, it is good idea to develop the reputation as someone to whom people can go for help **before** you ask others for their help.

8. Be a team player

Since so much of work is now accomplished through departmental or cross-functional teams, you must develop a reputation for being a solid and dependable team player. You can build such a reputation by volunteering for specific tasks, completing all tasks on time, and offering the leader helpful ideas in private, so it does not look like you are trying to run the team.

9. Talk the talk.

Understand the audience. For example, if you are trying to sell an idea to your boss, make sure you understand his or her communication style. Does he or she like lots of details of do you just need to hit the high points? What motivates him or her? Saving money? Customer service? Use organization jargon to point out how your idea addresses the points that motivate him or her.

10. Be flexible.

Business is all about change. Rather than complaining about it, anticipate and embrace it when it comes.

11. Become an expert in time management.

Put first things first. Consistently ask yourself, "What is the best use of my time right now?"

12. Build new skills.

As Eric Hoffer said, "Those who don't continue learning find themselves equipped to live in a world that no longer exists." See Rule 8 – Maintain Cutting Edge Skills on page 185 for ideas on skills to develop and how to develop them.

13. Hone your interpersonal skills.

Organizations are always looking for individuals who can get along with others. This is particularly true in today's environment of cross-functional teams.

Here are some ideas on how to maximize your interpersonal skills:

a. Be willing to help out.

In a time when many employees say, "That is not my job," you will stand out if you are willing to help others. As Zig Ziglar said, "You can get everything in life you want if you will just help enough other people get what they want."

b. Share credit.

If something does not work out well, most people are willing to point the finger at others. As the saying goes, "Victory has a thousand fathers, but failure is an orphan." You will win a lot of friends by acknowledging others' contributions.

c. Make the other person feel important.

No matter how busy you are, you must take the time to make the other person feel important.

—Mary Kay Ash

My friend, Michael, recently landed an executive position with a major company. After he had been with the company for a while he casually asked the CEO why he had chosen him over all of the other candidates. The CEO told Michael that all of the candidates were extremely qualified, but one thing that had set him apart from the others was that the janitor had recommended him. Then my friend remembered a chance meeting with the janitor in the elevator on the day he had come for his interview. Michael had been very pleasant with the janitor, asking how long he had worked there, and letting him brag about his granddaughter. It turns out that the janitor was good friends with the CEO's driver. The janitor had told the CEO's driver about his conversation with Michael, and the CEO's driver had told the CEO about the conversation.

The CEO told Michael the fact that he treated the janitor with dignity and respect told him that he would be a good fit for the organization.

    d. Remember names.

    As Dale Carnegie said, "Remember that a man's name is, to him, the sweetest and most important sound in any language."

    My wife was in the hospital and we met a nursing assistant named Maxine. The next time we were at the hospital several months later my wife saw Maxine and said "Hi Maxine." Needless to say Maxine was flabbergasted that my wife had remembered her name. A few minutes later, I came onto the floor, saw the nursing assistant and said, "Hello Maxine, how are you?" Maxine was so elated she went all over the floor telling anyone who would listen that both my wife and I had remembered her name. Needless, to say Maxine became our new best friend.

e. Become interested in others.

You can make more friends in two months by becoming interested in other people than you can in two years by trying to get people interested in you.

—Dale Carnegie

f. Talk about what the other person is interested in.

Since 1978, I have run a small business in which I sell advertising calendars. Year after year, the same customers buy calendars from me. I was with one customer recently because it was time for him to order his calendars – a very large order, I might add. I was asking him about his two favorite topics: his son and cars. He was willing to talk extensively about both.

As I was about to leave he said, "I really enjoy having you come by, maybe you could make it twice a year." Why do you think he would like me to come by twice a year? Why do you think that, despite numerous proposals from other calendar suppliers, he will only order his calendars from me? I think it is because we talk about the things in which he is interested.

g. Smile.

As Chuck Swindoll said, " I cannot think of too many times when a smile is inappropriate."

This poem by Rabbi Samson Raphael Hirsch points out the importance of a smile:

A smile costs nothing, but gives much.

It enriches those who receive it, without making poorer those who give it.

It takes but a moment, but the memory of it lasts forever.

None is so rich or mighty that he can get along without it, and none is so poor that he cannot be made rich by it.

A smile creates happiness in the home, fosters good will in business, and is the countersign of friendship.

It brings rest to the weary, cheer to the discouraged, sunshine to the sad, and is nature's best antidote for trouble.

Yet it cannot be bought, begged, borrowed or stolen, for it something that is of no value to anyone until it is given away.

h. Avoid using inflammatory words.

Instead of saying "You are confused" or "That's stupid" You might try, "I can see why you would believe that. In fact I used to think the same thing until……."

i. Use appropriate words when speaking to others.

When talking with bosses, use words and phrases that show a "can do" attitude. Examples are:

1. I accept full responsibility for the outcome.

2. If you approve, I will take the ball and run with it.

3. I am committed to finding the best solution.

4. We will have to use our creativity.

5. I look forward to working on this.

6. You make an excellent point.

7. I want to get your take on this before I proceed.

8. In order to meet the deadline, I will adjust my priorities.

9. In order to operate within the budget guidelines, I will consider all alternatives.

10. You can count on me to deliver a quality product in a timely manner and within budget.

When talking with colleagues, use words and phrases that show respect. Examples are:

1. It's in our best interest to collaborate.

2. If we cooperate, both of us can meet our deadlines.

3. May I borrow your idea?

4. Let's work together to develop a joint strategy.

5. I want to get your opinion.

6. I know you are experienced in this area.

7. A team effort is the best approach.

8. May I pick your brain?

When talking to subordinates, use words and phrases that show you value them.

1. I want to get your ideas before we develop the overtime policy.

2. How do you suggest we set up the work teams?

3. Let's formulate a strategy that meets the goal but is comfortable to us.

4. Are you aware of what we are trying to achieve here?

5. Would you please give this some thought and discuss it with me on Monday?

6. Do you see any flaws in the process we are considering?

7. What would you consider an appropriate form of recognition?

8. Perhaps I need to rethink my original decision.

j. Remember these career-enhancing words:

1. The six most important words: "I admit I made a mistake."

2. The five most important words: "You did a good job."

3. The four most important words: "What is your opinion?"

4. The three most important words: "If you please."

5. The two most important words: "Thank you."

6. The least important word: "I."

k. Be a good listener.

We listen all the time. Listening is natural. Is it? Let us do a quick listening self-assessment.

On a scale from 1 to 3, give yourself a score as follows: 1 = never, 2 = sometimes, 3 = very often.

The higher your score, the more effective you are as a listener.

Figure 3.3
LISTENING SELF-ASSESSMENT

Behavior	Score
I stop talking when someone is speaking to me.	
I look the person in the eye.	
I listen to the complete message without interrupting.	
I resist the temptation to finish the other person's sentences.	
I observe nonverbal clues.	
I ask open-ended questions to clarify my understanding of the message.	
Before stating my position, I make sure I understand the other person's point of view.	
I listen to other's point of view even if I think they are morons.	
I maintain an open mind.	
I do not allow potential distractions to capture my attention.	
Total (Add up your scores)	

If your score is: You are:
10 – 15   A non-listener.
16 – 23   A passive listener.
24 – 30   An empathetic listener.

Reasons people do not listen effectively.

1) They are not interested.

2) They are busy thinking of what they are going to say.

Studies show that the average person spends approximately 65 percent of the "listening" time thinking of what they are going to say. So they pretend to listen and assume that they understand.

3) Listening is hard work.

Since listening involves concentration, after listening you should feel tired. In fact studies show that effective listening increases both the pulse rate and the blood pressure.

4) They can listen faster than people can talk.

The average person can listen at a rate of 400 to 600 words per minute; most people speak at a rate of 200 to 300 words per minute. As a result, they sometimes take mental trips (daydream) and come in for landing occasionally. While they are away they could miss a key piece of information.

5) Information overload.

Several things compete for attention. Therefore, people sometimes put up a filter to block out things they don't need. In the course of doing that they may block out things they do need.

6) Bias.

They may have formed a bias against the other person based on previous encounters. They may consider the person a "whiner" for example.

7) They are busy.

They may be preoccupied with an upcoming meeting, getting to the in-basket, a report that is due, or any number of other issues.

Tips for effective listening:

1. Take appropriate nonverbal steps such as:

o   Turning down the music.

o   Putting your telephone on mute.

o   Facing the speaker.

o   Establishing eye contact.

o   Relaxing your posture.

o   Nodding.

2. Notice the words.

o   Words make up 7% of the message we receive.

3. Observe the body language.

o   Body language makes up the largest part (55%) of the message. (See Figure 3.4 on page 72 for some generally accepted meanings of various body movements in the American culture.)

4. Pay attention to the vocal tone.

o   This makes up 38% of the message.

> You have probably heard people say, "It's not what you said, it's how you said it". In fact, I can remember my mother saying to me "Young man, don't you use that tone of voice with me."

5. Ask open-ended questions.

> This allows you to probe for information, ideas and feelings. An example is: "Could you tell me more about why you believe your way would work better?"

6. Offer encouraging statements.

> Examples are "Uh-huh," "I see" or "That's interesting," "Tell me more," "It sounds like you have some definite ideas on the subject."

7. Let the person know you understand the facts.

> Say things like, "In other words, what you have decided is ...", or "If I understand you correctly you believe that..."

8. Let the person know you understand his/her feelings.

> Examples are "You felt left out of the loop" or "You feel that you had a better idea."

9. Summarize the key points.

> Ways to do that: "These appear to be your key concerns," or "You would like to see the following changes take place."

10. Avoid:

> a) Interrupting.
>
> b) Forming your response while the other person is still talking.
>
> c) Anticipating what the other person is going to say.
>
> d) Arguing.
>
> e) Judging.
>
> > Examples are "You shouldn't feel that way". "You are making a big thing out of nothing". "That is a dumb idea."

Rick Pitino, the former basketball coach at the University of Kentucky, tells a story that illustrates the importance of listening. According to Coach Pitino, when he went into the home of a young man he was trying to recruit, he had a routine. After a 45-minute presentation, he would talk to the recruit and his family about the strengths of the university.

He talked about the huge stadium in which they play their games, the academic programs, the support services, the training facilities–all the things that made the University of Kentucky the best. He was quite passionate in his delivery.

Afterward, the assistant coaches who had traveled with Coach Pitino complimented him on what a fantastic job he had done in selling the university. Yet, many times the recruit would say, "no thanks."

As Pitino watched how this unfolded time after time, he decided to change his approach. Instead of going into a recruit's home and immediately going into his sales pitch, he would ask the recruit, "What do you want in a college? In a basketball program?" He would ask the family, "What do you expect in a college?" Instead of doing most of the talking, Coach Pitino listened and showed interest in what the family wanted. Once he knew that, he would talk about how the university could meet those wants.

The assistant coaches were very confused. They said "Coach, you did not mention the stadium or the academic support." Coach Pitino would say, "I know."

But an amazing thing started to happen. Instead of being told, "no thanks," the University of Kentucky was usually among the families' top two choices. Why? Instead of going in and giving a standard presentation he listened and showed interest in what the family wanted. Once he knew that, he would talk about how the University could meet those wants.

Figure 3.4

BODY LANGUAGE

Behaviorists who study communication say these are examples of nonverbal message and the meaning they may convey in American culture.

1. FACE

o Maintaining eye contact - confidence and interest.
o Not maintaining contact - insecurity or lack of interest.
o Smile - Satisfaction.
o Stroking chin - Trying to make a decision, thinking.
o Raised eyebrow - Disbelief, surprise.
o Frowning - Disbelief, disagreement, does not understand.

2. ARMS

o Unfolded - Openness and honesty.
o Folded - Defensive, something to hide.

3. HANDS

o Firm handshake - You are glad to meet them, you are comfortable and confident with the situation.
o A light wimpy handshake - Lack of interest or insecurity.
o Making hand gestures - relaxed and confident.

Figure 3.4 – Page 2

BODY LANGUAGE

- o Clenched fist – anger or irritation.
- o Hand to cheek – evaluating, thinking.
- o Rubbing hands together – anticipation.
- o Standing with hands on hips – defiant, aggression.
- o Sitting with hands clasped behind head – confidence, superiority.
- o Tapping or drumming fingers – impatience.
- o Rubbing eyes – doubt, disbelief.
- o Rubbing nose – rejection, doubt, lying.
- o Open palm – sincerity, openness, innocence.

4. HEAD

- o Tilted – Interested.
- o Leaning forward - Interest.
- o Resting in hand – boredom.
- o Fast nod – I understand, move on.
- o Moderate nod – I think I understand, not sure.
- o Slow nod – I understand, but disagree.
- o Shaking from side to side – disagreement, disbelief.

5. LEGS

- o Sitting with legs crossed, foot kicking – boredom, nervousness.
- o Sitting with legs apart – open, relaxed.
- o Brisk, erect walk – confidence.

o   Walking with hands in pocket, shoulders drooped
    – dejection.
o   Locked ankles – apprehension.

ACTION PLAN

I will implement the following ideas:

1. _____.

2. _____.

3. _____.

4. _____.

5. _____.

4

Perform A Self-Assessment

The most successful people know themselves well and they move in the direction of their talents.

—Bud Bray,
Is it too late to run away and join the circus?

When it comes to career choices, many times the scenario looks like this: you need a job, you learn that the XYZ Company is hiring, you apply, go for an interview and get hired.

In other words, your career may have chosen you, instead of the other way around. It is not surprising, then, that a survey of 180,000 workers revealed that 80 percent of them did not like their job. As a result, there are three main days in the week:

o "Blue" Monday

o "Hump" Day (Wednesday)

o TGIF (Thank Goodness it's Friday)

In order to change (or better still, prevent) this scenario do a self assessment by answering questions 1 through 6 on pages 76 through 81. Use Figure 4.1 and 4.2 on pages 85 through 91 to help you answer the questions.

1. What skills do I have?

__Interviewing
__Solving problems
__Public Speaking
__Analyzing information
__Coordinating activities
__Conducting inspections
__Using computers
__Writing
__Working with numbers
__Organizing things
__Conducting research
__Planning
__Managing money
__Listening
__Supervising others
__Initiating action
__Building things
__Persuading others
__Building consensus
__Motivating others
__Making decisions
__Working with details

Place a checkmark next to all skills that apply.

Feel free to add skills to the list.

2. What skills do people compliment me on?

__Interviewing
__Solving problems
__Speaking in public
__Analyzing data
__Coordinating activities
__Performing inspections
__Using computers
__Writing
__Working with numbers
__Organizing things
__Conducting research
__Planning
__Managing money
__Listening
__Supervising others
__Initiating action
__Building things
__Persuading others
__Building consensus
__Motivating others
__Making decisions
__Working with details

Place a checkmark next to all skills that apply.

Feel free to add skills to the list.

It may be helpful to review your results from instruments such as Myers-Briggs or other assessments.

3. What are my personality traits?

__Supportive
__Responsible
__Tactful
__Resourceful
__Enthusiastic
__Organized
__Energetic
__Creative
__Charismatic
__Candid
__Analytical
__A quick learner
__Flexible
__People-oriented
__Optimistic
__Task-oriented
__Courageous
__ Logical
__Confident
__Team-oriented
__Competent
__Competitive
__Assertive
__A risk-taker
__Versatile

Place a checkmark next to all traits that apply.

Feel free to add traits to the list.

4. What do I love to do most?

As Malcolm Forbes said, "The biggest mistake people make in life is not trying to make a living at doing what they most enjoy".

—Helping others
__Inspiring others to reach their potential
__Developing new products or services
__Writing policy and procedures
__Solving complex problems
__Working with children
__Working with the elderly
__Marketing new products and services
__Building new structures

Place a checkmark next to all that apply.

Feel free to add to the list.

5. What do I value?

__Working close to home
__Helping others
__Being in a learning environment
__Performing the same tasks repeatedly
__Variety and change
__Job security
__Working independently
__Working as part of a team
__Working in a small company
__Working in a large company
__Having fun
__Working in a multicultural environment
__Having advancement opportunities
__An aesthetically pleasing environment
__Being recognized as an expert
__Competition
__Influencing others
__Having a sense of achievement
__Being creative
__Adventure and excitement
__A fast-paced environment
__Prestige and social status
__Taking risks
__Having authority

Place a checkmark next to all that apply.

Feel free to add to the list.

6. What are my hobbies?

"Work and play are words used to describe the same thing under different circumstances."

—Mark Twain

You can turn a hobby into a for-profit activity. For example, Jim Miller's hobby was planning celebration events. So he came up with the idea of putting together corporate picnics. Today he nets $1,500 to $7,000 per picnic. He has also written a 355 page manual called How to Start and Operate a Corporate Picnic Business which retails for $49.95.

In your spare time, do you enjoy:

—Painting
—Crafts
—Traveling
—Sewing
—Caring for animals
—Playing with computers
—Surfing the Internet
—Talking
—Fishing
—Shopping
—Playing with kids

Place a checkmark next to all that apply.

Feel free to add to the list.

7. Look for common threads among:

    a. Skills
    b. Things people compliment you on
    c. Personality traits
    d. Things you love to do
    e. Values
    f. Hobbies

For example, do you see yourself as being good at organizing things? Do people compliment you on your ability to organize things? Do your personality traits match those of what you consider an organized person? Do you love organizing things? Is being organized something you value? If you answered "Yes," you probably should pursue a position in which you get to apply your organizational skills.

What happens when you do what you were meant to do?

You will be eager to "get at it." Instead of saying TGIF (Thank Goodness it's Friday), You will say TGIM (Thank Goodness it's Monday) Let me give you some examples of what I mean:

According to Chuck, the only job he ever wanted was to be a waiter. When we go to the restaurant where he works, I often tell him that one of the reasons that I come there is to watch him as he serves his customers. You can just tell this is his true calling.

Bill Parcells had it made. As a retired football coach, all he had to do was travel from his New Jersey home to

Connecticut one day a week, sit in a television studio and provide expert analysis about football. He was paid well over a million dollars for doing this. However, after only a few months he concluded that he was born to be a football coach. He let it be known that he was interested in returning to the sidelines and he wound up as the head coach of the Dallas Cowboys. He said he feels alive again.

Maria began working part-time at a bank after school. She did so well that after graduation the management offered her a permanent position. Being an outstanding performer, she climbed steadily up the corporate ladder.

All the while, however, she knew this was not what she was meant to do. However, since she did not know what it was that she was supposed to be doing she continued with her banking career.

After doing some volunteer work as a caregiver, she concluded that this was what she was meant to do.

Having reached that decision, she resigned and enrolled in a nursing program. Today, she is on the verge of graduating at the top of her class and she has her pick of nursing assignments.

John Denver was asked to give the commencement speech at his old high school. He encouraged the graduating class to be themselves. "The best thing you have to offer the world is yourself", he said." He went on to tell them about how he had gone to Texas Tech to become an architect, but quit to become a singer. "Everybody said I was making a big mistake. I struggled to find opportunities at first. They turned me down for the shows at Six Flags. But I knew deep down inside, I knew I was born to sing for people. And singing is the most joyful thing for me. It's what's inside you that counts. And if it's not right for you, don't do it."

As you know, John Denver went on to record 14 Gold records and eight Platinum albums. He gave the world such songs as "Rocky Mountain High," Sunshine on My Shoulder" and "Thank God I'm A Country Boy." In 1996, he was inducted into the Song Writer's Hall of Fame.

Figure 4.1

PAID POSITIONS

(Complete in reverse chronological order)

Company _____

Position Title _____

Dates: From _____ to _____

Duties and responsibilities:
_____
_____
_____
_____
_____

Skills you used:
_____
_____
_____
_____
_____

Circle the skills you enjoyed using most.

Figure 4.1

PAID POSITIONS

(Complete in reverse chronological order)

Company _____

Position Title _____

Dates: From _____ to _____

Duties and responsibilities:

_____
_____
_____
_____
_____

Skills you used:

_____
_____
_____
_____
_____

Circle the skills you enjoyed using most.

Figure 4.1

PAID POSITIONS

(Complete in reverse chronological order)

Company _____

Position Title _____

Dates: From _____ to _____

Duties and responsibilities:

_____
_____
_____
_____
_____

Skills you used:

_____
_____
_____
_____
_____

Circle the skills you enjoyed using most.

Figure 4.1

PAID POSITIONS

(Complete in reverse chronological order)

Company _____

Position Title _____

Dates: From _____ to _____

Duties and responsibilities:

_____
_____
_____
_____
_____

Skills you used:

_____
_____
_____
_____
_____

Circle the skills you enjoyed using most.

Figure 4.2

VOLUNTEER POSITIONS

Organization _____

Position Title _____

Dates: From _____ to _____

Duties and responsibilities:

_____
_____
_____
_____
_____

Skills you used:

_____
_____
_____
_____
_____

Circle the skills you enjoyed using most.

Figure 4.2

VOLUNTEER POSITIONS

Organization _____

Position Title _____

Dates: From _____ to _____

Duties and responsibilities:

_____
_____
_____
_____
_____

Skills you used:

_____
_____
_____
_____
_____

Circle the skills you enjoyed using most.

Paddle Your Own Boat

Figure 4.2

VOLUNTEER POSITIONS

Organization _____

Position Title _____

Dates: From _____ to _____

Duties and responsibilities:

_____
_____
_____
_____
_____

Skills you used:

_____
_____
_____
_____
_____

Circle the skills you enjoyed using most.

ACTION PLAN

I will implement the following ideas:

1. _____.

2. _____.

3. _____.

4. _____.

5. _____.

5

Set A Goal

At this very moment you are WHO you are and WHERE you are because of what you've allowed to inhabit your goal-box.
—Richard Gaylord Briley

Imagine you are on a flight and the pilot comes on and says: "Good morning, ladies and gentlemen. This is your captain speaking. I have some good news and some bad news. The bad news is we have lost one engine and our direction finder. The good news is we have a strong tail wind and wherever we are going, we are getting there at a rate of 600 miles per hour. So sit back, relax and enjoy the trip."

I don't know about you, but I would not have an enjoyable trip. Yet, if you don't have a goal, you are like the passengers on that plane – directionless, lacking energy and being pushed along by the winds of circumstance.

Conversely, having a goal provides both direction and energy. As one author put it, "The mind will not reach toward achievement until it has a clear goal. Once you set the goal the switch is turned on, the current begins to flow and the power to accomplish becomes a reality."

Tips for setting goals:

1. Think Big.

As CEO Randy Sheparo said, "A key career stopper is setting your goals too low." Thinking big demands that you shake off self-limiting beliefs such as "I could never go back to school," and "They will never promote me," etc.

I like Les Brown's philosophy, "Shoot for the moon. Even if you miss you will land among the stars."

2. Set a preliminary goal.

This establishes **what you think you want**. It is preliminary because you will need to do some further investigation to determine if it is something **you really want**.

3. Put the goal in writing.

As Brian Tracey says, "Goals that are not in writing are not goals at all. They are merely wishes or fantasies." Let me give you an example of the impact of written goals. In 1953 researchers conducted a study of Yale University graduates. They asked the graduates two questions: "Do you have written goals?" and "Do you have a written plan for achieving your goals?" They found that less than 3 percent had written goals and a plan for achieving them. During a follow-up study in 1973, researchers interviewed all of the surviving members of the 1953 class. The results were shocking. They found that after 20 years the three percent of the graduates who had written goals and a plan for achieving them had a net worth higher that the combined net worth of the 97 percent of the graduates who did not.

When writing your goals:

a. Avoid using "weasel" words and phrases.

Instead of saying: "I hope to be promoted."

Say: "I will be promoted."

b. Say what you **want**, not what you **don't want**.

Instead of saying, "I want to get out of this terrible job." say: "I will be promoted to Senior Staff Analyst."

c. Make sure the goal is:

Specific – It spells out what you want.

Measurable – You can determine if you achieve it.

Achievable – You have a realistic chance of reaching it.

Relevant – It is related to your skills, what you love to do, and your values.

Time definite – It has a deadline. As Brian Tracy said, "Goals are dreams with deadlines".

For example: I will be promoted to Senior Staff Analyst by August 1, 2006.

4. Gather information to confirm the goal is something you want.

This step prevents you from spending a great deal of time pursing a goal that you really don't want after all. You can gather information by:

a. Reading position descriptions.
b. Reading vacancy announcements.
c. Visiting relevant Web sites.
d. Conducting informational interviews.

The purpose of an informational interview is to gain information about a position or organization in which you are interested. An added benefit is you meet new networking contacts.

Before the interview

a. Research the organization by visiting their Web site, reading financial reports and trade journals.

b. Identify a key contact within the organization.

c. Call the key contact and request 20-30 minutes to ask some questions to help you determine if this is a position you want to pursue. Make it clear that you want information, not a job.

d. Plan to dress as though you were going for a job interview.

This gives you an opportunity to make a good first impression.

e. Prepare your resume and carry it with you. (See questions 9 and 10 under "f" (below) to understand why it is important to do this.)

f. Prepare your questions in advance. Possible questions to ask include:

> 1) What does someone need to get into this profession? (Degrees, certifications, experience, knowledge, skills, etc.)

> 2) What will it take to succeed in this position in the future?

> 3) What do you like most about the position?

> 4) What challenges do you encounter? Staffing, budget, operational, other?

> 5) Describe a typical day.

> 6) What is the salary range?

> 7) What trends do you see emerging? Are things stagnant? Is there growth? Are there signs of decline?

8) What is the typical career path?

9) Would you look over my resume and offer suggestions?

10) May I leave a copy of my resume with you for future reference?

11) Would you recommend another contact that can provide additional insight?

Note: These are only suggestions. Feel free to substitute your own questions.

g. Practice your questions with a friend.

h. Call to confirm the appointment.

i. Plan to arrive at least 10 minutes early.

j. Plan to take extra copies of your resume in case the interviewee wants to keep a copy.

During the interview:

a. Greet the interviewee with a moderately firm handshake. Establish eye contact. Give a warm, enthusiastic smile.

b. Project enthusiasm.

c. Ask your questions succinctly.

d. Listen to the responses.

e. Ask follow-up questions, if appropriate.

f. Take notes.

g. Exchange business cards.

This gives you the correct spelling of the interviewee's name and address in order for you to send him or her a thank you card.

h. Respect the interviewee's time by ending at the agreed-upon time.

After the Interview:

a. Send a note within three days, thanking the interviewee for his her time.

b. You may want to conduct other interviews before finalizing your decision to pursue the position.

5. Decide that you want to pursue this position.

6. Make sure pursuing this position is consistent with your other goals.

For example, if one of your goals is to be at home with your family every night, you probably should not pursue a position that is going to routinely require you to travel out of town.

7. Identify the knowledge, skills and abilities required to achieve the position you are seeking:

a.

b.

c.

8. Determine how you will acquire the knowledge, skills, and abilities.

I will acquire the skills, knowledge and abilities through:

Work experience (Date)	I will complete by:

a.

b.

c.

Training (Date)	I will complete by:

a.

b.

c.

Education   I will complete by:
(Date)

a.

b.

c.

9. Identify potential obstacles and develop strategy for overcoming each one.

It is not a question of "if" but "when" you will encounter obstacles. As Frank Clark said, "If you find a road with no obstacles it probably does not lead anywhere." As an example, you may not have childcare while you attend evening classes. The key is to develop a way to overcome each obstacle.

OBSTACLES

Obstacle   How you will overcome   Complete by

10. Define, prioritize and set completion dates for all tasks necessary to accomplish your goal.

For example:

Task:	Complete By:
Update resume	10/1/2005
Identify target companies	10/5/2005
Attend Interviewing Skills Workshop	11/15/2005
Schedule interviews	12/1/2005
Evaluate job offers	2/1/2006
Begin new position	3/1/2006

11. Pick a "goal-model."

If you were planning to climb Mt. Everest, learn to fly an airplane, or become a parent you would probably look to someone who has successfully done it. The same holds true for reaching your career goal. So, rather than taking the advice of a friend, co-worker or fishing partner, seek out someone who has successfully done exactly what you are attempting to do. You may want to emulate what has worked for them and avoid the things that did not work.

12. Commit to paying the price.

"Success has a price tag, and the tag reads courage, determination, discipline, risk-taking, perseverance and consistency."

—James Meston

People generally fall into one or two categories. The first category is those who are **interested in being successful**. They engage in "Wishcraft". They say, "I Wish" I had another job. Then they say, "but I don't." So they never get a new job.

The second category is those who are **committed to being successful**. They say, "I will have a new job" and they commit to making it happen.

Kathleen is such a person.

She was a very successful restaurant manager. She had a nice salary and a generous benefits package. After some soul-searching, she decided that her real purpose in life was to be a nurse.

So Kathleen resigned from her comfortable position and enrolled in a two-year nursing program. Since her income was drastically reduced, she rented her house out in order to get money to pay for tuition, her mortgage and living expenses. In the meantime she rented a room in a friend's basement.

Kathleen understood that, as Joe Girard said, "The elevator to success is out of order. You'll have to use the stairs…one step at a time."

Are you "interested in being successful" or are you "committed to being successful"? There is a big difference.

Since every achievement comes with a cost, take a sheet of paper and draw a line down the middle. On one side of the line write "Costs" and on the other side of the line write "Benefits." List as many things as you can think of on either side of the paper. See Figure 5.1 on page 104 for an example.

Figure 5.1

Costs/Benefit Analysis Worksheet

Costs	Benefits
Must go back to school	Greater self-esteem
Will cost money	Improved job satisfaction
Will have to change lifestyle	Influencing organizational behavior
	Fulfilling life purpose
	Financial peace of mind

Based on the benefits, are you willing to pay the costs? If the answer is "yes" you are committed to being successful.

13. In order to target your self-promotion efforts, identify at least three organizations that have the position you are seeking.

_____

_____

_____

_____

14. Visualize success.

As Stephen Covey says, "Everything is created twice. There's a mental creation, and a physical creation." So, paint a picture in your mind of what it will look like when you achieve your goal. Picture yourself in your new role. Where are you? What does the environment look like? How are you dressed? Who are your customers? How do they react when you deliver your product or service? What does a typical day look like? Let us look at an example:

I am performing the following duties:

- o Meet with customers to do a needs assessment
- o Design curriculum that meets customer needs
- o Deliver workshops
- o Evaluate the effectiveness of workshops

Salary range: $57,000 - $68,000

Location: Baltimore/Washington area

Work hours: 8:00 – 4:00

Working environment
Physical facilities: Private office

Size of the organization: 20,000 – 30,000 employees

Co-Workers: I will be part of a training delivery team.

15. Get On With It.

"A lot of people have ideas, but there are few who decide to do something about them. The critical ingredient is getting off your butt and doing something. Not tomorrow, not next week, but today. It's as simple as that."

—Nolan Bushell, Atari founder

Gail understands this philosophy. She attended a two-day workshop I led at her agency. Midway through the second day, she approached me during a break and said she had really been inspired by the information I had presented. She went on to say she wanted to leave right then and get started on implementing her plan of action to become a manager. Of course, I agreed.

Six months later, I was leading a workshop for new managers at the same agency. Guess who was in the workshop? You're right. There was Gail, a newly appointed manger.

16. Stay focused.

Consider the postage stamp. It sticks to one thing until it reaches its destination.

—Josh Billings

No matter how excited you are about your goals, you can get distracted. Those distractions can come in many forms: people who want your attention, opportunities to pursue something that seems more lucrative, family, health or, financial issues, etc. Yet, if you are to be successful you must keep your focus on your goal.

Let's look at some examples of people who did just that:

Today, almost every one recognizes the name McDonald's. In fact, studies show that McDonald's is the second most recognized brand name, coming in right after Coca Cola. A new McDonald's opens somewhere in the world every 5 hours.

What you may not know is that the founder of McDonald's, Ray Kroc, could easily have been distracted by:

o   Health problems.

   He suffered from diabetes, arthritis, gall blander and thyroid problems.

o   Financial strains.

   He was deeply in debt and even had to mortgage his house to the maximum.

o   Holding down several jobs.

   In order to make ends meet he worked as a paper cup salesman, real estate broker, piano player, and milk shake mixer salesman.

Through it all he told himself "The best is ahead of me," and he kept his focus on the big idea – McDonald's.

Finally, at the age of 52, he sold his first hamburger.

Today, Evon Hallman is a college comptroller. In order to appreciate the significance of this you need to understand that:

- o It took her 10 years to complete her Bachelor's Degree.

- o During the time she was pursuing her degree she worked a full-time job.

- o She consistently had to change her work shift in order to attend classes.

- o She attended four colleges before completing her degree.

- o She was the primary caregiver for her mother during this time.

Like Ray Kroc, Evon had numerous opportunities to get distracted. Instead, she kept her eyes on her goal. As a result, when the comptroller position became available, there she was, with degree in hand; ready to step into this critical role.

How to stay focused:

a. Review your tasks and completion dates daily.

As the saying goes, "Out of sight, out of mind." Keep your goals and the list of tasks and completion dates in a place where you are constantly reminded of them and their importance. You might post a copy on the refrigerator, the dashboard of the car and the bathroom mirror.

b. Do something every day to move closer to your goal.

It may be having lunch with a member of your network, updating your resume, practicing your interview skills, researching a target organization's Web site, etc. But don't let a day go by without doing something to make progress toward your goal.

c. Recognize that you are giving up some small things in the short term in order to get some bigger things in the long term.

d. Continually ask the key question.

Every time you are about to make a decision ask yourself, "Does this take me closer to my goal?"

e. Celebrate achieving milestones.

As a means of providing motivation to continue pursuing your goal, celebrate achieving milestones along the way. As an example, when Evon Hallman completed the first semester of her degree program, she treated herself to a weekend at a health spa, with massages, a facial, a manicure and a pedicure.

17. Develop a "What if" strategy.

Change is inevitable, except from vending machines.

—Creative Wit

In order to prevent change from derailing your pursuit of your career goals, you must develop a strategy that answers three "what if "questions:

o   What if I decide I want to change employers?

o   What if I decide to take the plunge and become self-employed.?

o   What if I am laid off? (With staff reductions, mergers, acquisitions, downsizing, outsourcing, etc., this is a real possibility. According to the Department of Labor, each year more than 3.3 million people are laid off from their jobs.)

How to develop a "what if" strategy:

a. Get control of your finances.

There are several steps you can take to gain this control:

o   List all of your expenses.

o Look for things you can cut back on or eliminate altogether.

o Look for ways to save money on things that remain.

o Order a copy of my book, 425 Ways to Stretch Your $$$$. You can get a copy at **www.vernonwilliams.net**.

b. Live below your means.

Make it a family priority to live on less than your annual earnings.

c. Develop alternative sources of income.

As a youngster, I learned a valuable lesson as I helped my grandmother gather eggs. We always carried four baskets, even though neither of them was full. When I asked her why, she told me if we dropped a basket all of the eggs would not be crushed, since we had three others.

Although I would later become a well-paid corporate executive, I remembered that lesson. I did part-time consulting and taught seminars. When conditions changed and I was downsized, I transitioned to being a full-time consultant, workshop leader and author.

d. Network, network, network.

According to the Department of Labor, 48 percent of people got their job through word of mouth, i.e. a friend of a friend. This confirms the Theory of Six Degrees of Separation, which says there is a maximum of only five people standing between you and achieving your goal. Therefore, you should always be on the lookout for opportunities to build new relationships. You never know which friend of a friend is going to be able help you in your career pursuits. For further information, See Rule 7 – Identify, maintain and expand your network on page 173.

e. Go on interviews.

Make it a point to do this even if you are not interested in the position.

Marie is without peer as a pharmacist. She is very customer-focused and is well-liked by her manager. Yet, she told me recently that Friday would be her last day. She went on to say she had found another position that provided different challenges and did not require her to be on her feet for 12 hours per day, nor work nights or weekends. In addition, the new position came with a substantial pay increase. I asked her how this fantastic opportunity had come about. Marie said that, despite the fact that she liked her job, she had made it a point to contact executive search firms to let them know of her qualifications and interests. This usually resulted in her going on a couple of interviews per year. Well this time, an opportunity she could not refuse presented itself.

For further information on interviewing see Rule 6 – Master the art of self-promotion on page 117.

Delphine is a good example of someone who had an effective "what if" strategy.

She was a supervisor in the Information Technology department for a large company. Her long-term goal was to become an IT Director. While pursuing this goal, Delphine developed her "what if" strategy.

She began by listing all of her family's monthly fixed and variable expenses. Then she called a family meeting to discuss ways to eliminate or at least cut back on the variable expenses. As a family, they made a commitment to live below her salary. With the cutbacks on spending, Delphine was able to add to her "rainy day" fund.

In order to keep her interviewing skills sharp and to test her marketability, Delphine went on at least two job interviews per year.

Recognizing that many opportunities come by word of mouth, she kept in contact with people in her network while continuing to add new people.

As alternative income sources, Delphine purchased two rental properties. The rent covered the mortgage and repairs, plus provided some extra income, as well as a nice tax shelter.

In addition, she did computer programming through a

temporary agency on weekends and at night. Besides providing additional income, this helped keep her technical skills sharp.

One day, the word came down that the company had been bought out. Since the company that bought her company had its own IT department, Delphine's entire department was laid off and given a 90-day severance package.

While others fretted, Delphine was not worried. She knew that with her technical skills and contacts she would be OK. She took a three-month vacation. When she returned, she increased her hours at the temporary agency. Meanwhile, she continued to pursue her next position, one that would keep her on the path to becoming an IT Director.

ACTION PLAN

I will implement the following ideas:

1. _____.

2. _____.

3. _____.

4. _____.

5. _____.

6

Master The Art Of Self Promotion

The turtle lays thousands of eggs without anyone knowing,
but when a hen lays an egg the whole country is informed.

— Malayan Proverb

There is a popular misconception that the best opportunities
go to the best qualified people. In fact, the best opportunities
go to the people who are best at self-promotion. The
dictionary defines self-promotion as "the process of making
oneself more widely and favorably known." So, if you are
serious about achieving your career goals, you have to be
like a hen and "inform the whole country" of who you are
and what you have to offer.

How to become a master self-promoter:

1. Overcome the reluctance to "toot your own horn."

Many people are unwilling to promote themselves.
This may be because of:

> a. Fear of rejection.
> b. Feeling like they are intruding on others.
> c. Humility.

After all, as children, many of us were taught that
it is rude to talk about ourselves.

The good news is that you can overcome this reluctance.

Ask yourself these questions:

1) Do you have skills or knowledge from which others could benefit?

2) Do you enjoy helping others?

If you answered YES, think of yourself as someone seeking to serve others, as opposed to serving yourself.

2. Establish your career "brand".

What makes a consumer buy one product over another? The answer is marketing, or more specifically "branding". The dictionary defines "branding" as "the use of advertising, distinctive design, and other means to make consumers associate a product with a specific manufacturer." Companies such as Allstate ("You're in good hands") State Farm ("Like a good neighbor") and McDonald's ("I'm lovin' it") have mastered the art of branding.

Since you want employers to select you over other candidates, you, too, must develop a way for employers to associate specific characteristics with you - in other words you must "brand" yourself.   Your brand defines who you are, what you have to offer, what sets you apart from others, and describes the added value you provide. Here are some questions to help you identify your brand:

a. What are your skills? (Review Chapter 4 – Perform a self-assessment on page 75.)

b. To which organizations are you going to target your brand? (Review Chapter 5 - Set a Goal on page 93.)

c. What are the needs and interests of the target organizations?

d. How can you satisfy those needs and interests?

Having answered these questions, develop a benefit statement aimed at your target organizations. For example:

"I save IT managers time and money by delivering software development projects on time and within budget."

3. Align yourself with the "stars."

There is an old Italian saying that rings particularly true when it comes to self-promotion: "Dicami che andate con e vi dirò che siete." Translated literally, it says "tell me who you go around with and I'll tell you who you are." In other words, you are judged by the company you keep.

So, in order to enhance your brand, keep company with recognized high achievers.

4. Recruit your boss as part of your marketing team.

With his or her access to information and people, your boss is in a position to help advance your career. I say "in a position" because in order to tap into this assistance, you must convince him or her to be part of your team. You can do that by:

a. Letting your boss know your goals.

b. Identifying the benefits your boss could gain if you got promoted. Some possibilities are: a reputation for developing and advancing people, recognition from top management for developing people, (a key component in recruiting and retention of top employees)

c. Identifying your boss's "hot button" issues and developing creative ways to solve problems in those areas. Make sure your proposed solutions are well thought out and can save money, reduce staff, improve efficiency or improve customer service. Go a step further and volunteer to lead a task force to implement one of your ideas.

d. Seeking your boss's counsel on specific steps you can take to accomplish your goals.

e. Learning about his or her outside interests and hobbies and chatting with him or her about them in private.

f. Providing your boss with monthly updates on your accomplishments.

g. Updating your boss on any education or training you complete.

h. Updating your boss on any certifications you receive.

i. Offering to help your boss carry out some of his or her responsibilities, i.e. preparing a report, conducting an office meeting, responding to a customer complaint, etc.

j. Volunteering to help out other departments or teams. This shows your interest and desire to help your organization achieve its goals.

5. Dress for the job you want, not the job you have.

The way you dress is critical to your success. Regardless of your level, you want to project an image of competence, knowledge and professionalism. Here are some general guidelines that several professional wardrobe consultants say are appropriate for various situations.

Professional Dress

Women: Business suits, dresses, tailored separates, or skirts and blouses. Pants may be worn if they are part of a professional business suit with a jacket. Closed-heel and closed-toe shoes are recommended. Hair and make-up should be conservatively done. One piercing per ear. Avoid nose and other facial piercing.

Men: Conservative (medium to dark colors) business suits with an appropriate tie. Shirts should be white or blue.

Shoes should be well-polished. No visible body piercing.

Business Casual Dress

Women: Business suits, dresses, skirts and coordinated blouses, and casual pantsuits with jackets. Closed-heel and closed-toes shoes are recommended. Hair and makeup should be conservatively done. Sweaters, cardigans or contrasting vests. One earring per ear. Avoid nose and other facial piercing.

Men: High quality khaki or gabardine pants. Solid colored shirts and pullover sweaters are appropriate. Nice leather shoes (such as loafers) that are well-polished. Always wear socks.

Casual Dress

Women: Khaki pants with a blouse. Closed-heel and closed-toe shoes. Hair and makeup should be done conservatively. One piercing per ear. Avoid nose and other facial piercing.

Men: Khaki pants and oxford shirts. Always wear socks. Avoid body peircings.

As I mentioned, these are general guidelines. Look around.

Emulate the way successful people around you dress. You may want to contact your Human Resources department to get information on the dress code for your particular organization.

Let me give you an example of how dress can impact career goals. Victor started his new job as mailroom clerk. Having had experience as a retail buyer, his goal was to become a purchasing agent. Instead of wearing jeans, T-shirts and sandals like his colleagues, he wore a shirt and tie and always presented a well-groomed appearance. The executives immediately noticed him since he delivered mail throughout their floor. Within six months Victor was moved to the purchasing department as an assistant buyer. Fifteen months later he was promoted to a senior buyer position.

6. Develop a portfolio of your work.

Recognizing that "seeing is believing," artists and photographers use portfolios to demonstrate their work. Likewise, a portfolio is very effective for showcasing your work during interviews. You might include:

a. Articles you have written.

b. Awards you have received.

c. Brochures you have developed.

c. College transcripts and degrees.

d. Letters of commendation.

e. Letters of recommendation.

f. Merit reviews.

g. Training certificates.

h. Videos showing you in action.

i. Photographs.

j. Proposals you have made.

k. Manuals and handbooks.

l. Anything else you can print, frame, digitize or photograph.

7. Quantify, record and inform your boss of your accomplishments.

Focus on things such as:

a. Dollars saved.

b. Increased customer base.

c. Improved efficiency.

d. Increased sales.

8. Select a mentor.

Very few people get to the top without being taken under the wing of an older person somewhere along the way.

—Jean Paul Lyet

One recent study found that in four out of five cases, those promoted had a mentoring relationship with someone higher in the organization that helped them. Some organizations have formal mentoring programs, but even if yours does not, you should proactively seek out mentors.

A mentor can:

a. Serve as a role model.

b. Put you in touch with resources for ideas and information.

c. Introduce you to people who can help you advance your career.

d. Share knowledge about the organization – traditions, values, unwritten rules of how things really work.

e. Advise you on the best professional organizations to join.

f. Help you develop your skills.

g. Spread good words about you around the organization.

When selecting a mentor:

a. Take control of the process.

It used to be that a senior manager would seek out a younger employee, take him or her under his or her wing and show him or her the way around the organization. Rather than waiting and hoping that that happens, proactively select a mentor.

b. Pick someone you can trust, who is interested in you, has time to meet with you, is knowledgeable, and who is well-respected within the organization.

c. Do not limit yourself to one.

d. Since mentoring relationship do not last forever, you should continue to look for new mentors from whom you can learn.

9. Create your own opportunities.

Examine your organization's needs. Write a proposal for a new position that places you in charge of meeting a need. Even if your proposal is rejected, it shows your initiative.

10. Become "solution" focused rather "problem" focused.

Instead of pointing out problems to your boss, develop at least one well-thought out solution before discussing the situation with him or her. Problem-solvers get promoted. Complainers who expect the boss to solve all their problems simply get labeled as "whiners".

11. Become active in your industry association.

Attend conferences, serve on committees and panels. Volunteer to conduct a workshop.

12. Avoid "clockwatching."

If you work at a place that values "face time," make sure you put in as much time as those with whom you are competing. That may mean coming in early and staying late.

13. Keep a positive, "can-do" attitude.

See Rule 2 – Develop and maintain a positive attitude on page 27.

14. Make good use of business cards.

Keep a supply of business cards with you at all times and be ready to give them out.

15. Sign up for high profile projects.

Early in my corporate career, I volunteered to head up a major reorganization within our division. In this role, I gave a lot of presentations. During one presentation, there was a man in the audience from another department who liked my style. I wound up getting transferred to his department, which later led to my being promoted to a higher position.

16. Write articles for industry trade journals and your organization's newsletter.

You get to show off your writing skills and expertise to a wide audience. Someone in that audience may be looking for a person with your skills. Include a picture of yourself along with the article. Make sure your boss sees the article.

17. Take a Dale Carnegie course.

In addition to polishing your speaking skills, you get to do some networking. Once, while enrolled in a Dale Carnegie course, a class member who was an executive with another company offered me a job.

18. Look for opportunities to give presentations.

This gives you an opportunity to demonstrate your public speaking skills.

19. Conduct informational interviews.

In addition to gaining insights about positions, you also get to meet people and give them a copy of your resume. (See informational interviewing – Rule 5 on page 96.)

20. Head up the U.S. Savings Bond Drive, the United Way Campaign or the Combined Federal Campaign (CFC).

In addition to portraying yourself as a good corporate citizen, you get to meet lots of people who could potentially help you in your career pursuits.

21. Go on a temporary assignment to another department.

Since you will come into contact with other managers, it increases the likelihood that you will meet someone who likes you. That, in turn, will open up many new opportunities for promotion.

22. Serve on an interdepartmental task force.

You expand your network of acquaintances, learn more about how the organization works and rub elbows with new managers.

23. Network, network, network.

(See Rule 7 – Identify, maintain and expand your network on page 173.)

24. Ask satisfied clients for a letter of recommendation.

25. Target at least three departments that have the position that you want.

26. Use the direct approach.

Introduce yourself to a decision-maker in the department in which you want to work. Explain how you can help him or her accomplish his or her goals. Use your benefit statement. (See Branding, item 2 of this section)

27. Consider a lateral move.

Sometimes you may need to make a lateral move in order to position yourself to move up.

28. Speak up at meetings.

Meetings provide an excellent opportunity to get noticed. Come to meetings with fresh ideas for cutting costs, improving processes or solving problems.

29. Maintain an up-to-date resume.

Tips for demonstrating your value through your resume:

> **a. Prepare a "boiler plate" resume.**
>
> List all of the positions you have held, jot down titles and accomplishments. Once you have assembled this information, you can pick out the appropriate parts when applying for a particular position.
>
> **b. Do your homework.**
>
> Research the organization carefully before you submit a resume. Then tailor your resume to meet their needs. Use the organization's buzzwords.
>
> **c. Read the job announcement carefully.**
>
> This lets you know exactly what the hiring manager is looking for.
>
> **d. Use words wisely.**
>
> The key is getting the right information to the hiring manager in a fast, readable style. You can do that by using a minimum of words to provide maximum information. The following example uses too many words:
>
> *In this position, it was my responsibility to assist the program director on evaluating health care programs. Due to the fact that most of these centers*

were in rural areas, it was important that I traveled at least three days a week.

It's full of useless words and phrases that block the point, i.e. "due to the fact," "it was important," and "it was my responsibility."

Replace those with a stronger, easy-to-access message such as:

In this position, I assisted the program director in evaluating health care programs. Because most of these centers were in rural areas, I traveled at least three days a week.

e. Avoid repetition.

As this example shows, repeating information slows your message:

I worked with new law enforcement officers who were just entering the force and needed to learn techniques for identifying and interrogating suspects who they suspected of illegal activity. In my capacity, I trained them on these techniques.

Notice that "new law enforcement officers" and "who were just entering the force" say the same thing. So do "suspects" and "who they suspected of illegal activity" and "work with" and "trained".

Here is a better way of saying the same thing:

I trained new law enforcement officers on techniques for identifying and interrogating suspects.

f. Describe your experience with concrete rather than vague words.

Vague: *"responsible for managing and training"*

Concrete: *"managed a team of software engineers"*

g. Use words and phrases that define the level and scope of your experience and skills.

Examples are: "wrote complex documents," "prepared policy statements," "spoke before groups of 100 or more people," "managed multimillion dollar projects."

h. Use modifiers to define the frequency which you performed the tasks.

Examples are: occasionally regularly, annually, monthly, weekly and daily.

i. Use specifics when describing your work experience or skills.

Examples are names of software you use, i.e. Microsoft Word or Lotus 1-2-3.

j. Keep sentences short and clear.

Short, direct sentences help make your point. In the example below, the line is so long it practically leaves the reader out-of-breath:

My 12 years as a customer service representative have given me the opportunity to become comfortable speaking to virtually anyone and to answering questions calmly and professionally even when the person I am speaking to is upset.

By breaking up sentences, the point flows better. For example:

My customer service representative experience provided opportunities to sharpen my skills. For example, I am comfortable speaking to virtually anyone. I can answer questions calmly and professionally, even when the person I am speaking to is upset.

k. Make your message stand out.

Paragraphs that are easy-to-see are more than *nice* - they can make or break your message. Keep your paragraphs brief, usually between 5 and 10 lines. Put important points first - where they're most visible. Here are some possibilities:

1) Use short paragraphs.

While an associate editor for Agricultural Magazine, I selected each month's special features on scientific findings and agricultural economics; hired five new writers, all with scientific backgrounds; and reviewed all copy to ensure a style accessible to readers ranging from rural farmers to university researchers.

2) Use subheads.

While an associate editor for Agricultural Magazine, I was responsible for:

o *Critical content decisions.*

I selected each month's special features on the relationship between scientific findings and agricultural economics, among other articles.

o *Quality of articles.*

I reviewed all copy to ensure the style was accessible to readers ranging from rural farmers to university researchers

1. Focus on outcomes.

What is the most important aspect of your work experience? The answer may be a surprise: the outcome. In fact, you'd be amazed by how many people forget to mention this critical aspect of their experience. When discussing outcomes, be sure to discuss the *whats, the hows, and the scope of your experiences:*

1) What occurred?

Did you improve the workplace? Perhaps you refined technology tools, created programs or organized procedures. Regardless, let the hiring manager know *what* occurred. Use brief examples to best illustrate your point whenever possible.

2) How much and how many?

Did you start new projects? How many? Did you save your previous office money? Time? How much? Don't forget percentages, numbers and degrees that apply.

Notice how this example falls flat because it ignores the outcome:

As a supervisor at Early Start, I oversaw the development of grant proposals. While in this position, I put systems in place to ensure that my employees provided the government with the exact information it needed.

This revision is more revealing and competitive:

As a supervisor at Early Start, I oversaw a team of 10 employees who developed grant proposals. While in this position, I developed a template-based system to help my coworkers anticipate requirements. This helped us meet all deadlines a week in advance and create proposals that won us two grants more than the previous year.

m. Showcase your role.

Did you work on your own? As part of a team? In a supervisory capacity? As a team leader?

Describe your role in the projects. For example:

I helped put together conferences. Among my responsibilities were sending invitations, calling potential guests, and preparing the conference materials.

It would be stronger if worded this way:

As part of a team of five employees, I helped put together conferences. Among other responsibilities, I coordinated with my coworkers to send invitations, call potential guests, and prepare the conference materials.

Were you promoted while working on a project? If so, mention that too. Note, for example, this response doesn't mention a promotion:

In my last position, I spent 2 to 3 months at a time in the field collecting samples for the study. The following year, I spent most of time in the lab, only going to the field occasionally.

This revision is better:

In my position as Project Manager, I spent 2 to 3

months at a time in the field, overseeing 5 specialists who assisted me in collecting samples for the study. I was promoted to Senior Project Manager which required that I spend more time in the lab. As a result, I went to the field only occasionally

n. Mention timeframes.

Address these questions: What were the dates or lengths of time you worked on a project or job? Did you work full-time or part-time? If part-time, what percentage of your time did you spend on that work? For example, this candidate could have worked in his position for a few months as a part-time employee:

I served as a contractor for the agency. I regularly produced educational videos and IVT training sessions.

The response is more strongly worded if stated as follows:

From 1999-2002, I served as a full-time contractor for the agency. I spent at least 30% of my time producing educational videos and IVT training sessions.

If you didn't spend substantial time in a particular position, include the dates anyway. Other information such as the outcome of your experience or the scope of your work will underscore its value.

o. Use show and tell.

Telling about your experience is great but be sure to use examples, too. See how this candidate's job sounds pretty blasé:

As a maintenance mechanic, I often worked in settings that required that I maintain control of every move in the operation.

Look at the difference a few specifics can make:

As a maintenance mechanic, I often worked in settings that required me to maintain control of every move in the operation. For example, for 16 months I worked on renovation projects in the Smithsonian Institution where I moved priceless museum exhibits using forklifts, cranes, skids and rollers.

p. Highlight personal traits.

In addition to job skills, employers look for personal and professional traits in job candidates. Below are some of the top traits:

1. Ambitious

2. Good communication skills

3. Success-driven

4. Enthusiastic

5. Reliable

6. Determined

7. Goal-oriented

8. Level-headed

9. Flexible

10. Confident

11. Detail-oriented

12. Loyal

13. Problem solver

14. Honest

15. Poised

16. Self-controlled

17. A self-starter

q. Resist additions.

Resist the temptation to send copies of awards, publications, training certificates, letters of recommendation, lengthy job descriptions, writing samples or a photo unless the hiring manager specifically requests it.

r. Use KSAs.

KSA stands for:

Knowledge – An organized body of information obtained through education or previous experience, e.g., biology, accounting, etc.

Skills - A manual, verbal or mental trait that is directly observable, quantifiable and measurable, e.g., typing.

Abilities – The aptitude to perform an observable activity which results in a product or consequence, e.g., ability to communicate orally.

KSAs are designed to show that you not only meet the basic requirements, but that you have what it takes to excel in the position.

When you submit your application for a position, the person reviewing that application will not infer your specific abilities and accomplishments from your resume. The KSAs provide you an opportunity to expand on the skills you've listed in your resume and give specific examples of your experience.

Steps to writing effective KSAs

Step 1: Gather information about yourself.

o   Employment background.

o Accomplishments (concrete evidence that proves your knowledge, skills, and abilities).

    o Did you resolve a long-standing problem?

    o Did you discover a new and better approach for getting things done?

    o What was solved, created, changed for the better or improved because you were there?

    o Did you take on any extra responsibilities above and beyond your job description?

    o What have your supervisors commended/ cited/awarded you for?

o All of the training and education you have received.

o All training and education you have provided.

o Special assignments, details, team responsibilities and acting positions.

o Publications, products, or research to which you contributed, either as part of a team or independently.

o Presentations and briefings you have made, whether in-house to key people, to other agencies, or at conferences.

o   Honors/awards (within the past three years).

o   Performance appraisals (they serve as "memory joggers" for your accomplishments).

Step 2: Learn as much about the position as possible.

Step 3: Compare the KSAs with the vacancy announcement and the position description.

Classify each "duty and responsibility" according to which KSA it reflects.

Step 4: Match your skills to the KSA requirements. List all related experience, accomplishments, education, training, and honors/awards that directly relate to each KSA.

Step 5: Follow the CCAR method in writing your KSAs:

CCAR stands for:

Challenge. Describe a specific problem or challenge you faced.

Context. Talk about the individuals and groups you worked with, and/or the environment in which you worked, to tackle the particular challenge (e.g., clients, co-workers, members of Congress, shrinking budget, low morale).

Action. Discuss the specific actions you took to address the challenge.

Result. Give specific examples of the results of

your actions. These accomplishments demonstrate the quality and effectiveness of your leadership skills.

Example of the CCAR Model:

C-Context.

I had a client who had some administrative support employees who were not motivated to take responsibility for their career.

C-Challenge

The employees had a negative attitude toward the agency. They refused to take responsibility for their career and blamed their supervisors for their failure to achieve their goals.

A-Action

I conceived, developed and taught a two-day workshop to help the participants identify barriers to their success, set goals and develop strategies for achieving those goals.

R-Result

Supervisors reported that employees' job performance improved. Eighty percent of the employees completed an Individual Development Plan that outlined a career goal and the specific steps (along with dates) that they needed to take in order to achieve their goal. The supervisors deemed the program such a success that they implemented it throughout the agency.

Tips for writing effective KSAs:

o   Review the vacancy announcement to see if KSAs are to be written in the resume or can be written on separate sheets.

o   Use clear, concise sentences.

o   Take between one half and one full page.

o   Give at least one example per KSA

o   Make every example different for each KSA statement.

o   Use a consistent length and format.

o   Use first person pronouns (I organized...)

o   Spell out terms before using acronyms

o   Use information from both paid and volunteer experience.

o   Describe results in specific quantities.

o   Be specific about your role in the organization or on a project. Describe if you assisted, managed, supervised, lead, or were a team player on a project

o Use wording from the duties section of the job vacancy announcement.

o Use action words when describing your experiences.

o Describe recent education and training that enhanced your skills.

o Include volunteer experience if it demonstrates your qualifications.

o Include relevant special assignments (e.g., details, task forces, committees).

o Include awards that relate specifically to the position.

o Highlight job-related training, skills, certificates, licenses, honors, awards, professional affiliations, leadership activities, etc.

o Be truthful.

30. Prepare a Cover letter for your resume

Although a cover letter is generally not required, using one gives you an opportunity to indicate your interest in - and passion for - the position. It also enables you to highlight your expertise and qualifications, demonstrate your knowledge of the organization, and finally, to showcase your potential value as an employee. An effective cover letter has four paragraphs:

Paragraph 1: Outlines the reasons for submitting cover letter.

"I am submitting my application for the position of training specialist."

Paragraph 2: Describes relevant qualifications for the position.

"My relevant qualifications for the position are nine years of results-producing experience in a variety of settings."

Paragraph 3: Describes how you can help the hiring manager.

"I can help you achieve your goals because I am thoroughly familiar with OSHA requirements and I can hit the ground running and be productive immediately."

Paragraph 4: Offers to come for an interview:

I am available to come in for an interview anytime that is mutually convenient.

31. Develop top-notch interview skills.

The purpose of an interview is for you and the prospective employer to further evaluate each other.

There is an adage that interviews are sought, dreaded then endured. With the proper preparation, an interview need not be dreaded or endured. As the saying goes, "Preparation and planning prevent poor performance."

Tips for a successful interview:

Before the interview:

a. Learn as much as possible about the organization.

This step is crucial because it enables you to tailor your responses to meet the organization's needs. You can gain this information by talking to current and former employees, customers and suppliers, and by reading periodicals, financial reports and visiting the organization's Web site.

b. Learn as much as possible about the position.

You can gain this information by carefully reading the job vacancy announcement and by talking to current and former employees.

c. Believe that you are the best candidate for the position.

If you don't believe you are the best candidate, stay home.

d. Assess your strengths and weaknesses.

Do you tend to speak too softly, or too rapidly, fidget and say "uh" a lot? Practice answering the questions without showing these weaknesses. Remember: practice does not make perfect, perfect practice makes perfect.

e. Make extra copies of your resume.

The interviewer may have misplaced the copy you sent or he/she may want to give a copy to a colleague. In addition, be sure to have a copy to which you can refer during the interview.

f. Review your resume to make sure you are intimately familiar with what you have written.

Pay particular attention to jobs you have held, and accomplishments you have made. This allows you to give examples and to elaborate without having to rely totally on your memory.

g. Prepare questions to ask.

An interview is generally viewed as a one-way street. This is not so. You want to ask questions as well as answer them because you want to make sure that there is a good fit.

Some questions you might want to ask are:

> 1) What are you looking for in the ideal candidate?

> 2) Could you give me a current job description for the position?

3) Who would be my supervisor?

4) What do you consider the major challenges facing the organization?

h. Review your features and benefits.

A feature tells what you can do. A benefit answers the question "Why is that important?"

Let's look at some examples:

Feature: I have 10 years of experience.

Benefit: That means I can contribute to your success immediately since I will need minimal training.

Feature: I can type 80 words per minute.

Benefit: I will speed up your work flow.

Feature: I am an excellent communicator.

Benefit: That will lead to higher productivity since employees will not waste time trying to figure out what they are supposed to do.

Feature: I am results-driven.

Benefit: That will enable you to please your boss.

Feature: I am dedicated.

Benefit: I will help you achieve your organization's mission.

i. Identify and coach your references.

Before making a hiring decision, most employers want to speak with people who know a candidate well. You should contact three to five people who will agree to provide favorable recommendations about you to future employers.

Always ask permission of the people before including their names on your reference list. The people you ask to be references should obviously be familiar with your abilities. Supervisors from either paid or unpaid jobs, teachers, coaches, advisors, and coworkers are all good choices for references. Select the most willing, articulate people you can. When people agree to be references, help them to help you. Give them a copy of your resume or application to remind them of your important accomplishments. Tell them what kinds of jobs you are applying for so they know what types of questions to expect.

After choosing and contacting references, type a list providing their names, addresses, telephone numbers, and relationship to you. Bring copies of this list with you to interviews.

k. Identify and develop answers to questions the interviewer may ask you.

Following are some typical questions you could be asked, along with some sample answers:

Question #1: Tell me about yourself.

This is an opportunity to talk about your qualifications, skills, experience and education that are relevant to the position. Use a maximum of two minutes. Don't ramble.

Sample Answer:

I am a highly energetic and enthusiastic trainer with ten years of experience and a unique ability to plan, develop and conduct courses. I am particularly adept at assessing clients' needs and implementing a flexible approach for meeting those needs. I have a proven record of being a direct and candid communicator with strong leadership characteristics. I have a masters degree in Psychology.

Write Your Answer Here:

_____
_____
_____
_____
_____
_____

Question #2: What are your strengths?

Choose at least three words/phrases that portray you in a positive light.

Sample Answer:

I am very organized, I am a team player and I have excellent platform skills.

Write your answer here:

_____

_____

_____

_____

_____

Question #3: What do you know about our organization?

This is an opportunity to demonstrate the amount of research you have done.

Sample Answer:

I know that you are the industry leader in the area of_____. I know that you are in the process of kicking off a campaign to _____ _____and that you just received a federal grant to study the effects of _____ _____.

Write your answer here:

_____

_____

_____

_____

_____

Question #4: Where do you see yourself in five years?

Be sure to include this company in your plans. Since the company will make an investment in you, they want to feel like you are committed to being with them.

Sample Answer:

I see myself growing and learning, taking on more responsibility here at the ABC Company. I would eventually like to move up in the organization to an even more responsible position such as _____
_____. (Name a specific position in the company.)

Write your answer here:

_____

_____

_____

_____

_____

Question #5: Tell me about a problem you solved in your last job.

Relate it to a similar problem that you might encounter in this position.

Sample Answer:

This is an opportunity to use the CCAR method.

C-Context

I had a client whose administrative support employees were not motivated to take responsibility for their career.

C-Challenge

The employees had a negative attitude towards the agency. They refused to take responsibility for their career and blamed their supervisors for their failure to achieve their goals.

A-Action

I conceived, developed and taught a two-day workshop to help the participants identify barriers to their success, set a goal and develop strategies for achieving the goal.

R-Result

Supervisors reported that employees' performance improved. Eighty percent of the employees completed an Individual Development Plan that outlined a career goal and the specific steps (along with dates) that they needed to take in order to achieve their goal. The supervisors deemed the program such a success that they implemented it throughout the company for all administrative support employees.

Write your answer here:

_____

_____

_____

_____

_____

Question #6: What did you like about your last job?

Talk about things that are key elements of the job you are seeking.

Sample Answer:

Since I am very customer-focused I liked the fact that I was able to meet with clients, assess their needs, identify their expectations and develop programs that met those expectations.

Write your answer here:

_____

_____

_____

_____

Question #7: How have you kept up with the changes that have occurred in your field?

This is an opportunity to talk about degrees attained since you began your career, seminars you have attended, self-study, rotational assignments, certifications, etc.

Sample Answer:

I recently completed a degree in Instructional Technology by attending courses in the evening. As a member of the American Society of Training and Development, I have taken advantage of the member discount and attended at least three workshops per year for the last five years. In addition, I subscribe to Training Today Magazine, which provides cutting-edge information on what's happening in the industry.

Write your response here:

_____

_____

_____

_____

_____

Question #8: Why should we hire you?

Sample Answer:

I am a highly energetic and enthusiastic trainer with ten years of experience and a unique ability to plan, develop and conduct courses. I am particularly adept at assessing clients' needs and implementing a flexible approach for meeting those needs. I am a direct and candid communicator with strong leadership characteristics. I have a master's degree in Psychology.

I am thoroughly familiar with all of the OSHA requirements and can become a productive member of your team immediately.

Write your answer here:

_____

_____

_____

_____

_____

Question #9: What are your career goals?

Point out how this position is part of your overall goal.

Sample Answer:

My goal is to continue to develop my skills as a trainer and administrator. My ultimate goal is to become a director of training here at ABC Company. That will give me the opportunity to impart some of what I have learned over the years to other people who are entering the profession.

Write your answer here:

_____

_____

_____

_____

_____

Question #10: What appeals to you about this position?

Sample Answer:

It gives me the opportunity to continue to grow and contribute to an organization that is recognized as a leader in the industry.

Write your answer here:

_____

_____

_____

_____

_____

Question #11: Tell me about one of your weaknesses.

Be honest. Everyone has weaknesses. However, talk about a weakness that has nothing to do with your ability to perform the functions of the position for which you are being interviewed.

Sample Answer:

If the position requires using existing computer programs, you could say, "I have superb skills when it comes to using Excel and Word. However, if you need actual programming done, I would need additional training."

Write your answer here:

_____

_____

_____

_____

Question #12: Who would give you a good reference and what would they say?

Stress the attributes that are important in the position for which you are being interviewed. You need to be sure to coach your references on what they should say if called upon.

Sample Answer:

If you talk to my former boss, Jack McDowell, he will tell you that I am a highly energetic and enthusiastic trainer. He will also tell you that I am customer-focused and that I am particularly adept at assessing clients' needs and implementing a flexible approach for meeting those needs. Finally, Mr. McDowell will tell you that I am a direct and candid communicator with strong leadership characteristics.

Write your answer here:

_____

_____

_____

_____

_____

Question #13: What are your strengths?

Sample Answer:

I manage time well and I am very cost-conscious. For example, in my last position I was asked to analyze the office communication system and to develop a recommendation to improve it. I completed the analysis two weeks ahead of schedule and made a recommendation to upper management that saved the company 20% on the communication system.

Write your answer here:

_____

_____

_____

_____

_____

Illegal questions:

It is illegal for the interviewer to ask you questions related to sex, age, race, religion and marital status. If you are asked such a question, you might gently point out that you see no relationship between that question and the qualifications that you bring to the position.

Once you have developed your answers, have a friend or relative ask you the questions so you can practice giving your responses. Videotape the session and critique your performance.

During the interview:

The interview begins the moment you arrive. Everyone you meet, from the receptionist to the hiring manager, will form an impression of you. Executive coaches say you have 3 – 7 seconds to make a favorable impression.

To ensure you make a positive impression:

1. Present a neat, well-groomed appearance.

2. Keep your head up and your shoulders back. This projects confidence.

3. Establish eye contact.

4. Use a firm handshake.

5. Wait to be invited to sit.

6. Sit up straight.

7. Face the interviewer directly. This projects alertness and focus.

8. Smile.

9. Keep arms and legs uncrossed. This is a sign of openness, that you have nothing to hide.

10. Don't fidget.

11. Speak clearly. Use correct grammar.

12. Answer questions concisely.

13. Lean forward at times to show you are engaged.

14. Relate your experience, education and training to the specific position

15. Don't just talk about your qualifications. Give lots of examples to demonstrate your competence.

16. If you don't understand a question, ask for clarification. "Excuse me, do you mean in my former job or are you talking about what I would do in this job"?

17. Never, never, never bad-mouth a former employer.

18. Highlight your features and benefits (See page 149).

19. Before leaving the interview, make sure you understand the next step in the selection process. Find out whether there will be another round of interviews, whether you should provide additional

information, and the timeframe within which a selection will be made. Finally, be sure to thank the interviewer. If you are interested in the job, say so.

20. Get the correctly-spelled name, address and telephone number of the interviewer.

After the interview

1. Ask yourself what went well.

2. Ask yourself what did not go well.

3. Send a brief thank-you letter within 24-48 hours of the interview.

Most thank you letters have three main paragraphs.

The first paragraph is your chance to thank the interviewer for meeting with you and to show enthusiasm for the job. You may refresh the interviewer's memory by mentioning the date of the interview and the position for which you applied.

The second paragraph is for you to briefly reiterate a few skills that make you well suited for the job. You might also mention a topic from the interview that was especially interesting to you. Also, include any important information you forgot to mention during the interview.

The third paragraph is where you thank the interviewer again, give your phone number, and state that you look forward to hearing from him or her.

Write or type the letter on solid white, off-white, or gray stationary. Use a standard business format. Put a colon after the interviewer's name and a space after each paragraph. Don't forget to sign your first and last name.

Many employers say an e-mailed thank you letter is acceptable if e-mail correspondence was exchanged between the interviewer and the candidate. Otherwise, do not use an e-mail message.

Address the letter to the person who interviewed you, and make sure to spell his or her name correctly. If a group interviewed you, write either to each person you spoke with or to the person who led and coordinated the interview, mentioning the other people you met.

Finally, be sure to proofread the letter, and ask someone else to proofread it for you, too. Interviewers tell tales of misspelled, misused words written in thank you letters that tarnish the image of an otherwise impressive candidate. As you write your thank you note, remind yourself that you might be writing to your next supervisor.

See Figure 6.1 - Sample Thank You Letter on page 166.

4. Follow up with a telephone call within two weeks to:

    o   Determine if the hiring manager has reached a decision. If not,

    o   Determine if you are still under consideration.

    o   Restate your interest and qualifications.

    o   Ask if they have additional questions for you.

    o   Find out why, if you were not selected.

Figure 6.1 - Sample Thank You Letter

John Ryan
15 Spring Road
Hamlet, LS 41112
555-555-5555

August 25, 2006
Ms. Susan Carson
Director
Hamlet Child Development Center
Hamlet, LS 41112

Dear Ms. Carson: (Spell the interviewer's name correctly)

(Thank the interviewer) Thank you for the opportunity to interview with you yesterday afternoon. I am very interested in the childcare position you described.

(Highlight your qualifications) My child development classes, summer jobs, and recent volunteer work as a storybook reader at the community center have prepared me well for a preschool teaching position. I am especially interested in the field trip program you mentioned. I would welcome the opportunity to contribute to that effort.

(Express interest in the job) I enjoyed meeting you and your staff and look forward to hearing from you soon. If I can provide any additional information, please call me at (555) 555-5555. (Place your phone number near the end) Thank you again for your time and consideration.

Sincerely,

John Ryan

John Ryan

See Figure 6.2 - Powerful verbs and phrases to use in resumes, cover letters and interviews on page 168.

Figure 6.2

Powerful verbs and phrases to use in resumes, cover letters and interviews

- abated
- abolished
- accelerated
- accomplished
- achieved
- actively participated
- administered
- advanced
- advised
- analyzed
- applied
- assumed a key role
- authored
- automated
- built
- hired
- closed
- coached
- co-developed
- co-founded
- collected
- co-managed
- communicated
- completed
- computerized
- conceptualized
- conducted
- consolidated

- contained
- contracted
- contributed
- controlled
- convinced
- coordinated
- cost effectively created
- critiqued
- cut
- dealt effectively
- decreased
- defined
- delivered
- designed
- developed
- directed
- doubled
- earned
- eliminated
- emphasized
- enforced
- established
- evaluated
- exceeded
- executed
- exercised
- expanded
- expedited

Figure 6.2 - Page 2

Powerful verbs and phrases to use in resumes, cover letters and interviews

- facilitated
- filled
- focused
- formulated
- fostered
- founded
- gained
- generated
- headed up
- helped
- identified
- implemented
- improved
- increased
- initiated
- innovated
- instituted
- instructed
- integrated
- interviewed
- introduced
- investigated
- lectured
- led
- leveraged
- maintained
- managed
- marketed
- motivated

- negotiated
- orchestrated
- organized
- outmaneuvered
- overcame
- oversaw
- penetrated
- performed
- permitted
- persuaded
- planned
- played a key role
- positioned
- prepared
- presented
- prevented
- produced
- profitably
- promoted
- proposed
- prospected
- protected
- provided
- published
- quadrupled
- ranked
- received
- recommended

Figure 6.2 - Page 3

Powerful verbs and phrases to use in resumes, cover letters and interviews

- recruited
- reduced
- removed
- renegotiated
- replaced
- researched
- resolved
- restored
- restructured
- reversed
- satisfied
- saved
- scheduled
- scoped out
- selected
- self-financed
- set up
- sold
- solved
- staffed
- started
- stopped
- streamlined
- substituted
- supervised
- taught
- tightened
- took the lead in
- trained
- trimmed
- tripled
- turned around
- upgraded

ACTION PLAN

I will implement the following ideas:

1. _____.

2. _____.

3. _____.

4. _____.

5. _____.

7

Identify, Maintain and Expand Your Network

Few people are successful unless a lot of other people want them to be.

—Zig Ziglar

According to the U.S. Department of Labor, people get jobs in the following ways:

o 5 percent through the "open" job market (help-wanted ads on the Internet and in print publications)

o 24 percent through contacting companies directly (the cold-contact method)

o 23 percent through employment agencies, college career-services offices and executive-search firms

o 48 percent through referrals (word of mouth)

Since nearly half of all jobs are acquired through word of mouth, you must concentrate your efforts on getting as many people as possible involved in helping you achieve your career goals. This means "networking," which is defined as "building or maintaining informal relationships, especially with people whose friendship could bring advantages such as job or business opportunities."

Among other things, people in your network can give you job leads, offer advice and provide information about a particular company or industry. They may also introduce you to others who can provide leads or offer advice.

How to become a master "networker":

1. Identify your existing network by considering:

        a. Current fellow employees.

        b. Previous fellow employees.

        c. Customers/clients.

        d. Neighbors.

        e. Vendors/service personnel.

        One time, as I was preparing to conduct a workshop, the facility coordinator came by to make sure the room was set up properly. We struck up a conversation and she asked me if I promoted all of my workshops or if I used others to set them up. I told her that I set them up myself, but I preferred to simply show up and conduct the workshop. She gave me a contact name at a company that sets up conferences around the country. I contacted the conference company and we are working on ways we can collaborate.

f. Church members.

Let me give you an example of how I saw this work recently:

Janice had completed her degree but had not been able to find a job in her field. She kept sending in applications only to get the "Don't call us, we'll call you" response. One day during Bible study, a woman asked Janice's mom how Janice's job search was going. Janice's mom said it was not going very well. It turned out that a woman in the Bible study was a vice president at a large company that was looking for someone with Janice's skills. Janice went for an interview, was hired almost immediately and continues to work at that company. What makes the story even more amazing is that Janice had already applied and been turned down by the same company that eventually hired her.

g. Family and friends.

On another occasion, as I was doing a presentation for an organization. I recognized a woman in the audience. She is the sister-in-law of my wife's sister's best friend. I had not seen this lady for a number of years, but I remembered her immediately. She kept giving me that "I know this guy from somewhere look." During a break, I went over and introduced myself to her. She immediately remembered me and later contracted me to do several workshops over a two-year period.

h. School and university contacts.

Your college alumni association can be a fertile source of contacts.

i. Professionals (accountant, doctor, lawyer, auto repair technician, etc.)

When Kelly was out of a job, she mentioned it to her accountant. Her accountant had another client who was looking for someone with Kelly's skills. As a formality, Kelly went for an interview. She was hired on the spot.

j. Contacts from social organizations.

Fraternities and sororities.

k. Contacts from professional and trade associations.

2. Organize your network.

It is important to organize your network so you can follow up with people in a systematic fashion. It doesn't matter what system you use, as long as it works for you. I use a database in which I enter key information (names, titles, company names, addresses, phone numbers, email addresses, and dates of communication). See Figure 7.1 on page

177 for an example. I have seen other people collect business cards and write notes and comments about their network.

Figure 7.1 - Network Database

Name	Title	Company	Address	Telephone #	Email	Contact Dates

3. Maintain your network.

Having identified and organized your network, you must maintain those relationships in order to be able to tap into them as needed.

a. Make sure you are clear on your specific goals.

(Review Rule 5 – Set a Goal on page 93)

People will feel like you are wasting their time if you ask them for help in finding a job but you are not clear on exactly what type of job you want.

b. Keep in touch with your network members.

It is extremely important to stay in touch with your network, especially when you do not need them. People do not want to feel like the only time they hear from you is when you want something. You can keep in touch by phone, email or "snail mail"

(U.S. Postal Service). You can also send birthday, anniversary, get well and holiday cards.

Former President Bill Clinton was a master at this. While in college he began keeping 3"x5" cards on people he met as he traveled. He kept in touch by sending them a birthday card just to let them know he was interested and also to let them know what he was doing. By the time he got ready to run for his first office he had 10,000 people with whom he had kept in touch. These became known as FOB (Friends of Bill) Imagine the potential for stuffing envelopes, putting up signs, making donations etc. But that is not all. All of those people knew people, and those people knew people. The numbers become staggering. Given those numbers, one can begin to understand how a poor boy from Hope, Arkansas could become President of the United States.

c. Have lunch at least once per month with a network member.

Catch up on what is happening with them and let them know what is happening with you.

d. Give freely of yourself.

There is an old saying, "If you are all wrapped up in yourself, you are overdressed." So look for opportunities to help others. For example, if you see an article in the paper or you come upon some information that might be helpful to another person in your network, pass it on. If you can refer them to someone who can help them, by all means do so.

e. Ask for new referrals.

As you make contacts, ask, "Who else do you know who might be able to help me land a position as an IT Specialist?" Try to get two or three referrals from each person.

f. Follow through.

If someone is kind enough to give you a referral, follow through on it by contacting the source. Get back to the person who gave you the referral and let them know what happened.

g. Send thank you notes.

Always send a thank you note.

4. How to grow your network:

a. Be a conversation starter.

Whenever you find yourself around people, start a conversation. This could be in the elevator, in restaurants, in the bank, at the gym, the beauty salon, at the grocery store, at Little League games, etc. Every one you meet has the potential to help you accomplish your goals. The key to being a conversation-starter is preparation.

Some terrific (and safe) conversation starter questions relate to compliments, work and background questions.

1) Compliments

Observe an individual and look for something about which you can offer a sincere compliment. Examples are a person's outfit, a piece of jewelry or hair style. An example might be if you saw someone wearing a particular type of T-shirt and you said, "I see you are a Texas Longhorn fan."

2) Work

Questions such as where they work, what they do, what led them to that field and what they enjoy most about it are safe questions because people are willing to talk freely about these things.

3) Background

Background questions are a good way to engage people in a conversation. For instance, asking where someone grew up and where they went to school are quick and easy ways to begin a conversation.

b. Initiate informational interviews.

One of the best ways to gain more information about an occupation or industry – and to build a network of contacts in that field – is to talk with people who are currently working in the field. The purpose of the informational interview is to obtain information, not to get a job. For more on informational interviews, see Rule 5 – Set a Goal on page 96.

c. Join Toastmasters

Since some people are shy about networking, Toastmasters offers a non-threatening place to improve your public speaking skills while making valuable contacts. Toastmaster chapters are all over the world, so you can find one near you by checking your local newspaper or phone book.

d. Never leave home without business cards.

Since you never know when an opportunity might present itself, make sure you have a supply of cards at all times. I met someone at a family reunion who was instrumental in my getting a large training contract. As I am leaving the house, my wife always asks me if I have business cards.

e. Put a benefit statement on your business card.

The statement should explain how people benefit from doing business with you. As an example yours could say:

"I save IT managers time and money by delivering software development projects on time and within budget."

Another option is to use a catchy slogan. Once, when I was an independent sales representative for commercial printers I used the slogan "We print everything but money." People loved it and remembered me. It led to a lot of business.

f. Record comments on the cards you receive.

Don't just give out business cards, ask others for theirs. Once you receive a card write comments on the card such as the date and location you met, common points of interests, birthdays, anniversaries, hobby clubs, and other key information. These comments will prove valuable when following up with that person.

g. Join business and professional associations.

Attend conferences, serve on committees and panels. Volunteer to conduct a workshop.

h. Ask a question or make a point at a meeting.

Often you will find that someone shares your point of view or had a similar question. This can lead to a more in-depth conversation during a break.

ACTION PLAN

I will implement the following ideas:

1. _____.

2. _____.

3. _____.

4. _____.

5. _____.

8

Maintain Cutting Edge Skills

The only job security is to be more talented tomorrow than you are today.

—Michael Levin, Levin Communications

Some years ago, one could expect to work at the same job with the same organization, using the same set of skills, for his or her entire career without worrying about those skills becoming obsolete. That is no longer the case. Whether you are in accounting, administration, information systems, law, operations, marketing/sales or purchasing, organizations are looking for people with an ever-changing variety of skills to help them cope with the rapidly-changing global economy. That means you must be a lifelong learner. If not, you will quickly become obsolete.

How to become a lifelong learner:

1. Conduct an annual check-up of your skills to see how they match the skills employers seek most often.

The most sought-after skills are:

a. Using computers to acquire, organize, analyze, communicate and process information.

b. Problem-solving

1) Recognizing that there is a discrepancy between what is and what should be.
2) Identifying possible reasons for the discrepancy.
3) Devising and implementing a plan of action to resolve the discrepancy.
4) Monitoring and evaluating the results.
5) Revising the plan of action if necessary.

c. Negotiating

1) Listening to and reflecting on what has been said.
2) Clarifying problems and resolving conflicts.
3) Adjusting quickly to new facts/ideas.
4) Proposing and examining possible options.
5) Making reasonable compromises to resolve divergent interests.

d. Teamwork

1) Working cooperatively with others.
2) Contributing ideas, suggestions, and effort.
3) Doing your share of tasks necessary to complete a project.
4) Encouraging team members by listening and responding appropriately to their contributions.

5) Building on individual team members' strengths.
5) Resolving differences for the benefit of the team.
7) Taking personal responsibility for accomplishing goals.

e. Working with cultural diversity

1) Understanding one's own culture and how it differs from other cultures.
2) Understanding concerns of members of other ethnic and gender groups.
3) Respecting the rights of others.
4) Basing impressions on individual performance, not stereotypes.

f. Communication -

1. Writing

a) Communicating thoughts, ideas, information, and messages in writing.
b) Composing and creating documents such as letters, directives, manuals, reports and proposals; using language, style, organization, and format appropriate to the subject matter, purpose and audience.

c) Checking, editing and revising for correct information, appropriate emphasis, form, grammar, spelling, and punctuation.

2. Speaking

Organizing and verbally communicating messages that are appropriate to listeners and situations.

3. Listening

Receiving, interpreting, and responding appropriately to verbal messages and other cues such as body language in ways that are appropriate to the purpose.

g. Interpersonal

a) Demonstrating understanding, friendliness and adaptability.

b) Demonstrating empathy and politeness in new and ongoing group settings.

c) Relating well to others.

d) Responding appropriately as the situation requires.

e) Taking an interest in what others say and do. Mitigating conflict.

h. Planning/organizing

Designing, organizing and implementing a project within time and budget guidelines.

i. Serving customers

a) Actively listening to customers to avoid misunderstandings.
b) Identifying customers' needs.
c) Working and communicating with customers to satisfy those needs.

j. Creative Thinking

Using imagination freely, combining ideas or information in order to identify new possibilities.

k. Decision Making

a) Generating alternatives.
b) Evaluating each alternative.
c) Choosing the alternative that best meets the goal and is within time, budget, legal, operational and other constraints.

l. Leadership

Leading co-workers in carrying out team projects, even without organizational authority.

m. Analytical Skills

    a) Assessing a situation.

    b) Identifying the key aspects necessary in order to bring about the desired results.

n. Foreign language

Since business is now global, the ability to read, write and speak a second language will become more and more of a priority. Learning a second language such as Chinese or Japenese will increase your value to your current or future employer.

2. Take steps necessary to build skills

There are a number of ways to do this:

a. Seminars and workshops sponsored by:

    1) Your organization.
    2) Local colleges or universities.
    3) Professional organizations.
    4) Private companies such as Skillpath, Fred Pryor Seminars, National Seminars Group, The Learning Tree, etc.

b. Online courses.

These courses range from brief workshops and tutorials to degree programs. You can join these classes by paying a fee and accessing the designated Web site at the appropriate time.

c. One-on-one coaching.

You can hire a professional coach to come to your home or meet with you at another mutually convenient place. The coach tailors lessons to your needs.

d. Distance learning programs.

These programs provide a viable option to the traditional classroom setting. They are extremely flexible and can range from your communicating with teachers via email, audiotapes and teleconferencing to telecourses ("real time" broadcasts or videos) or interactive classrooms (you are electronically linked to the site) to traditional correspondence courses where you get and return course materials by mail.

e. Rotational assignments to other departments.

f. Volunteering outside of work.

g. Informal apprenticeships.

Sometimes called "shadowing," this involves following someone around who is performing the duties you want to learn.

h. Working on a special project.

i. Serving on a committee or task force.

j. Attending conferences.

Go to lectures provided by experts. You may even earn continuing education units.

k. Reading the latest books.

Check Amazon.com or the local bookstores to see the latest books that address your field.

l. Subscribe to trade publications.

m. Check Web sites that pertain to your field.

Many of them offer tips that you can use immediately in your job.

ACTION PLAN

I will implement the following ideas:

1. _____.

2. _____.

3. _____.

4. _____.

5. _____.

Paddle Your Own Boat

9

Keep Up-To-Date On Happenings In Your Field

The future belongs to those who prepare for it.

—Ralph Waldo Emerson

Which are the top companies? What are the latest products and services? What new laws or regulations have been enacted or under consideration? What are the latest trends? As an example, some companies have begun to operate 24 hours per day, 7 days per week. Whereas this used to only involve assembly line workers, it is becoming more prevalent among college-educated, technical support employees. This arrangement allows a U.S. technical person who works at night to provide technical support to a customer who calls from Tokyo during his or her lunch hour.

By 2007, companies are expected to spend $103 billion annually in outsourcing. This represents an 11 percent increase from the $61 billion that companies spent in 2004.

Being aware of this type of information helps you prepare for future opportunities with your current employer, or make a smooth transition to a new employer, if necessary.

How to keep up:

1. Subscribe to industry and trade publications.

2. Join industry trade associations.

3. Subscribe to Internet newsgroups that focus on your industry.

4. Surf the Internet, which is a knowledge repository. Some of the more popular sites are:

www.careermag.com
www.workforce.com
www.defense-aerospace.com
www.nytimes.com/pages/technology

5. Join Internet chat groups.

6. Read the local newspaper.

7. Attend company-sponsored seminars.

8. Further your education at local universities.

9. Network with colleagues.

10. Pay attention to what is happening around you.

In so doing, Eddie is an example of an employee who positioned himself to take advantage of some upcoming changes.

As an elementary teacher, he looked around and noticed

that many of the principals were about the same age. He further noted that several of them would be retiring within the next 7 - 10 years.

Eddie enrolled in graduate school to get a master's degree in education administration. Since the school system had no tuition reimbursement plan, he paid for it himself. Other teachers thought it was silly for Eddie to do this. Eddie also volunteered to prepare some reports to help his principal out, attended workshops for administrators, and selected a mentor.

In seven years, when the mass exodus began, Eddie was prepared. Consequently, he was named the first African American principal in the school district.

ACTION PLAN

I will implement the following ideas:

1. _____.

2. _____.

3. _____.

4. _____.

5. _____.

10

Persevere

Even the woodpecker owes his success to the fact that he keeps pecking away until he finishes the job he starts.

—Coleman Cox

The dictionary defines "persevere" as "to continue steadily in action or belief, usually over a long period, despite difficulties and obstacles."

I know lots of people who "tried" to get a promotion, start a business or get a degree. I say "tried" because they quit as soon as they met some difficulty. Carole, a woman I met recently, is a good example. She had been pursing a promotion for a few years. Despite the fact that she had repeatedly made the best qualified list, she never got promoted. During our conversation, no matter what strategy I suggested that she try, Carole was not hearing any of it. She had made up her mind that she was simply not going to get promoted, so there was no point in trying. You see, Carole had quit.

I love the story about a high school basketball coach who was trying to motivate his players to persevere through a difficult season. Halfway through the season he called his team together and said, "Did Michael Jordan ever quit?" The team responded, "No!" He yelled, "What about the Wright Brothers? Did they ever give up?" "No!" the team responded. "Did Walter Payton ever quit?" Again the team yelled, "No!" "Did Elmer McAllister ever quit?"

There was a long silence. Finally one player was bold enough to ask, "Coach, who's Elmer McAllister? We never heard of him." The coach snapped back, "Of course you never heard of him - he quit!"

On the road to achieving your career goals you must keep three very important things in mind:

1) It may take a while.

2) There are going to be times when you are tempted to quit.

3) If you quit, no one will ever hear of you.

Since failure can only happen when you quit, perseverance and failure cannot coexist.

How to avoid quitting:

1. Focus on the pay-off you will receive by achieving your goal.

Examples of pay-offs may include satisfaction, financial freedom, higher self-esteem, feeling of being in control, etc.

2. Picture yourself having achieved your goal.

3. Draw encouragement from people who resisted the temptation to quit and went on to achieve their goal.

People like:

- o Michael Jordan who, despite being told he was not good enough to make his high school team, went on to become perhaps the greatest basketball player of all time.

- o Henry Ford, who went bankrupt twice before making it big in the automobile business.

- o Thomas Edison

Everyone knows he invented the light bulb. What most people do not know is that Edison failed 9000 times before he perfected the light bulb. When asked how it felt to have failed 9,000 times Edison said "I don't feel like I failed 9,000 times. In fact, I succeeded in finding 9,000 ways not to make a light bulb".

- o Winston Churchill

He suffered through many political defeats before finally becoming Great Britain's prime minister. Despite the fact that Germany had a superior force in World War II, he rallied the spirit and the action of a nation on the way to becoming recognized as a world leader.

In his later years, he was invited to give the commencement address at Oxford University. Following his introduction, he rose from his seat, walked to the lectern, and simply said, "Never, never, never give up." Then he sat down.

o   Tyler Perry

Today, just the mention of his name in an advertisement as playwright and/or actor practically guarantees a sellout in several major markets. However, it was not always that way. Having been abused as a child, he wrote a series of letters to himself, trying to find a catharsis for his own childhood pain. He later wrote a play called, "I Know I've Been Changed," a rousing stage play about adult survivors of child abuse. The play mixes comedy and drama to help him recover from childhood scars. He took his last twelve thousand dollars and moved to Atlanta with a script in his hand and a dream in his heart. He rented a theater and put on the show.

Only thirty people showed up for the entire weekend.

During the next six years, Perry would become homeless. Broke and starving, but yet holding on to his faith, he believed that it would all come out all right one day. He kept saying "I know the Lord will make a way!

Just at the point that he was about to give up, he decided to do one last show and that faithful decision would change his life forever. The performance opened at the House of Blues in 1998 and sold out eight times over. Two weeks later, the play would go to the Fox Theater and sell out two shows.

"I Know I've Been Changed," went on to gross several million dollars. To date, another show, "Woman, Thou Art Loosed" has grossed over $5 million in the last five months, selling out in every major city and performing to standing room only crowds.

4. Learn a lesson from those who quit.

Just as we can learn from those who did not quit, we can also draw inspiration from those who did.

There is a story involving the California gold rush about two brothers who sold all they had and went prospecting. Immediately they discovered a vein of shining ore, staked their claim and proceeded to dig to get the gold ore out of the mine.

At first everything went well, but then just as quickly as the gold ore had appeared it disappeared. The brothers continued to dig for a while, but finally they decided it was no use. So they quit.

They sold all of their equipment and rights to the mine for a few hundred dollars and returned to their home back east.

The man who purchased the claim from them hired an engineer to examine the rock strata of the mine. The engineer advised the new owner to continue digging in the very same spot the previous owners had left off.

After digging three feet the new owner struck gold. He became wealthy beyond his wildest dreams.

If the two brothers had not quit they, instead of the new owner, would have been wealthy.

Don't Quit

When things go wrong, as they sometimes will,
When the road you're trudging seems all uphill,
When the funds are low and the debts are high,
And you want to smile, but you have to sigh,
When care is pressing you down a bit,
Rest, if you must, but do not quit.

Life is queer with its twists and turns,
As every one of us sometimes learns,
And many a failure turns about,
When he might have won had he stuck it out;
Don't give up, though the pace seems slow–
You may succeed with another blow.

Often the goal is nearer than
It seems to a faint and faltering man,
Often the struggler has given up,
When he might have captured the victor's cup,
And he learned too late when the night slipped down,
How close he was to the golden crown.

Success is failure turned inside out–
The silver tint of the clouds of doubt,
And you never can tell how close you are,
It may be near when it seems so far,
So stick to the fight when you're hardest hit–
It's when things seem worst that you must not quit.

– *Anonymous*

ACTION PLAN

I will implement the following ideas:

1. _____.

2. _____.

3. _____.

4. _____.

5. _____.

Index

Glossary

Body language – Mannerisms, facial expressions, and postures and can be interpreted as unconsciously communicating one's feelings or state of mind.

Blue Monday – The dreaded first day of the week for employees who are unhappy in the job.

Branding – The use of advertising, distinctive design and other means to make consumers associate a specific product with a specific manufacturer.

Clockwatcher – One who is eager to leave work as soon as possible.

Distance Learning – Training in which there is no face-to-face contact between the trainer and the trainees. Instead materials are provided remotely by means such as email, the Internet and correspondence.

Downsize – To reduce the size of a business or organization, especially by cutting the workforce.

Expert – One who has a great deal of knowledge about, or skill, training and experience in a particular field or activity.

Features vs. benefits – A feature is a fact. A benefit answers the question, "So What."

Goal Model – One who has accomplished a goal and others look to that individual for inspiration.

Hump Day – The name people who don't like their job call Wednesday. It signifies that there are only two more days until the weekend.

Informal apprenticeship – See "Shadowing"

Informational interview - Unlike an interview to get a job, an information interview is designed to gather information to help determine indeed one wants to pursue a particular job.

KSAs – Knowledge, Skill and Abilities

- o Knowledge – Mastery of facts, or information pertaining to a subject matter area.

- o Skills – Proficiency or competence in a particular area

- o Abilities – Demonstrated performance using knowledge and skills

Mentor – A senior or experienced person who gives guidance and training to less experienced person

Myers-Briggs – An instrument for measuring a person's preferred way of living his or her life.

Networking - Building or maintaining informal relationships, especially with people whose friendship could bring advantages such as job or business opportunities.

Organizational savvy – Understanding the informal rules of how an organization "really" works

Outsource – To buy labor or parts from outside the business rather than using the business' staff or plant.

Portfolio – A representation of one's work.

Problem-focused – Centering attention on pointing out problems rather than developing solutions.

Professional obsolesce – A condition in which one's skills are outdated and therefore useless.

Resource network – A group of people to who one can turn for assistance in accomplishing one's job duties.

RIF – Reduction in force

Rotational assignment – A temporary assignment to a position other than one's primary one.

Self-promotion – Making oneself more widely and favorably known.

Shadowing – Employee A follows Employee B around to determine a particular job suits him or her. Employee A may even perform some of the duties to get first hand experience.

Snail mail – Mail sent through the postal service.

Solution-focused – Centering attention on developing solutions rather than pointing out problems

TGIF – Thank Goodness it's Friday.

TGIM – Thank Goodness it's Monday.

Team Player – One who sacrifices personal interest in order to achieve a common goal.

Victor – A winner in a contest or battle.

Victim – A person who experiences misfortune and feels helpless to remedy the situation.

Wishcraft –Wishing that conditions were different from what they are, but never taking action to change the condition.

Work portfolio – A collection of samples of one's work in order to showcase one's skills. Examples are articles, awards, letter of appreciation, photographs, merit reviews, training certificates, videos.

Suggested Reading

Anderson, Nancy. *Work with Passion: How to Do What You Love for a Living*, New World Library, 2004

Augustine, Rosemary, How *to Live and Work Your Passion and Still Earn a Living,* Blue Spruce, 2003

Barnes, Leesa, *Schmooze Your Way to Success*, Savia Lane, 2005

Buckingham, Marcus, and Clifton, Donald O. Now, Discover Your Strengths, Free Press, 2001 Discover

Covey, Stephen, *7 Habits of Highly Effective People*, Simon & Schuster, 1990

Damp, Dennis *Take Charge of Your Federal Career*, FEND, 1998

Drake, Tim, *Wearing the Coat of Change: Handbook for personal Survival and Prosperity in the Unpredictable World of Work*, Texere Publishing, 1998

Edler, Richard, *If I knew then what I know Now*, Berkley Books, 1997

Embree, Marlowe, *Self-Managing Your Career*, Trafford, 1999

Farren, Caela, *Who's Running Your Career*, Bard Press, 1997

Fellman, Wilmer, *Finding a Career that Works for You*, Specialty Press, 2000

Ferrazzi, Keith, *Never Eat Alone, and other Secrets to Success, One Relationship at a Time*, Doubleday, 2005

Fisher, Anne, *Six Ways to Supercharge Your Career, Fortune,* 1997

Gale, Linda, *Discover What You Are Best At*, Fireside, 1998

Haray, Keith, *Who Do You Think You Are?* Harper Collins, 1994

Harrell, Keith, *Attitude Is Everything*, Hay House, 2004

Herriott, Peter, *The Career Management Challenge*, Sage Publications, 1992

Hill, Napoleon, *Keys to Success*, Simon & Schuster, 2000

Jolley, Willie, *A Setback is A Setup for A Comeback*, 2003

Keirsey, David, *Please Understand Me*, Prometheus Nemesis Press, 1998

Leider, Richard, *The Power of Purpose*, Berrett-Koehler, 1997

McGraw, Phillip, *Life Strategies*, Hyperion, 1999

Patterson, Tom. *Living the Life You Were Meant to Live,* Thomas Nelson, 1998

Phillipson, Ian, *How to Market Yourself: A Practical Guide to Winning at Work*, How to Books, 1995

Porter, Shirley, Porter, Keith, Bennett, Christine, *Me, Myself, and I*, Impact Publications, 1998

Ramsey, Dave. *The financial Peace Planner*, Penguin Books, 1998

Sandler, Mel, Gray, Muriel *Winning at Work*, Davies-Black, 1999

Schein, Edgar, *Career Anchors*, Pfeiffer and Co., 1993

Sheerer, Robin , *No More Blue Mondays*, Davies-Black, 1999

Sher, Barbar, *Wishcraft: How to Get What You Really Want*, Ballentine Books, 2004

Sinetar, Marsha, *Do What You Love, the money will Follow: Discovering Your Right Livelihood*, Dell Publishing, 1987

Tieger, Paul, and Tieger, Barbara, *Do What You Are*, Little, Brown, 2001

Troutman, Kathryn, *The Federal Resume Guide*, Jistworks, 1999

Wendelton, Kate, *Targeting the Job You Want*, Career Press, 2000

Whitcomb, Susan, *Resume Magic: Trade Secrets of A Professional Resume Writer*, Jistworks, 2003

CPSIA information can be obtained
at www.ICGtesting.com
FFOW02n1525151015
17713FF